DAVID HAIG

David Haig's plays include *My Boy Jack*, *The Good Samaritan* (Hampstead Theatre) and *Pressure* (Royal Lyceum Edinburgh, Chichester, Park Theatre and West End.) *My Boy Jack* was filmed for ITV, starring David, Daniel Radcliffe, Carey Mulligan and Kim Cattrall, and broadcast in 2007. *Pressure* was filmed in 2025, starring Andrew Scott, Brendan Fraser, Damian Lewis and Kerry Condon (produced by Working Title and Studio Canal), and released in 2026 in the USA and UK.

On stage, his distinguished acting career includes *Pressure* (West End) and *Rosencrantz and Guildenstern are Dead* (Old Vic). He won the Olivier Award for Best Actor for *Our Country's Good*, and received nominations for *The Madness of George III*, *Donkeys' Years*, *Guys and Dolls* and *Mary Poppins*. He has worked extensively in the West End, at the National Theatre, RSC and Royal Court Theatre.

His TV and film appearances include *Eloise at the Plaza*, *Etoile*, *Cobra*, *Downton Abbey* (film), *The Thick of It*, *Talking Heads*, *My Boy Jack*, *Two Weeks Notice*, *Four Weddings and a Funeral* and *The Thin Blue Line*.

Other Titles in this Series

Chiara Atik
POOR CLARE

Stephen Beresford
FANNY & ALEXANDER *after* Bergman
THE LAST OF THE HAUSSMANS
THE SOUTHBURY CHILD
THREE KINGS

Chris Bush
THE ASSASSINATION OF KATIE HOPKINS
with Matt Winkworth
THE CHANGING ROOM
CHRIS BUSH PLAYS: ONE
A DOLL'S HOUSE *after* Ibsen
FAUSTUS: THAT DAMNED WOMAN
HUNGRY
JANE EYRE *after* Brontë
THE LAST NOËL
OTHERLAND
ROBIN HOOD AND THE CHRISTMAS HEIST
with Matt Winkworth
ROCK / PAPER / SCISSORS
STANDING AT THE SKY'S EDGE
with Richard Hawley
STEEL

Jez Butterworth
THE FERRYMAN
THE HILLS OF CALIFORNIA
JERUSALEM
JEZ BUTTERWORTH PLAYS: ONE
JEZ BUTTERWORTH PLAYS: TWO
MOJO
THE NIGHT HERON
PARLOUR SONG
THE RIVER
THE WINTERLING

Alexi Kaye Campbell
ALEXI KAYE CAMPBELL PLAYS: ONE
APOLOGIA
BIRD GROVE
BRACKEN MOOR
THE FAITH MACHINE
THE PRIDE
SUNSET AT THE VILLA THALIA

Caryl Churchill
BLUE HEART
CHURCHILL PLAYS: THREE
CHURCHILL PLAYS: FOUR
CHURCHILL PLAYS: FIVE
CHURCHILL: SHORTS
CLOUD NINE
DING DONG THE WICKED
A DREAM PLAY *after* Strindberg
DRUNK ENOUGH TO SAY I LOVE YOU?
ESCAPED ALONE
FAR AWAY
GLASS. KILL. BLUEBEARD'S FRIENDS.
IMP.
HERE WE GO
HOTEL
ICECREAM
LIGHT SHINING IN
BUCKINGHAMSHIRE
LOVE AND INFORMATION
MAD FOREST
A NUMBER
PIGS AND DOGS
SEVEN JEWISH CHILDREN
THE SKRIKER
THIS IS A CHAIR
THYESTES *after* Seneca
TRAPS
WHAT IF IF ONLY

David Haig
THE GOOD SAMARITAN
MY BOY JACK
PRESSURE

Lucy Kirkwood
BEAUTY AND THE BEAST
with Katie Mitchell
BLOODY WIMMIN
THE CHILDREN
CHIMERICA
HEDDA *after* Ibsen
THE HUMAN BODY
IT FELT EMPTY WHEN THE HEART
WENT AT FIRST BUT IT IS
ALRIGHT NOW
LUCY KIRKWOOD PLAYS: ONE
MOSQUITOES
NSFW
RAPTURE
TINDERBOX
THE WELKIN

Conor McPherson
THE BRIGHTENING AIR
COLD WAR *after* Paweł Pawlikowski
DUBLIN CAROL
GIRL FROM THE NORTH COUNTRY
with Bob Dylan
McPHERSON PLAYS: ONE
McPHERSON PLAYS: TWO
McPHERSON PLAYS: THREE
THE NEST *after* Franz Xaver Kroetz
THE NIGHT ALIVE
PORT AUTHORITY
THE SEAFARER
SHINING CITY
UNCLE VANYA *after* Chekhov
THE VEIL
THE WEIR

Winsome Pinnock
THE AUTHENTICATOR
LEAVE TAKING
PIG HEART BOY *after* Malorie Blackman
ROCKETS AND BLUE LIGHTS
TAKEN
TITUBA

Jack Thorne
2ND MAY 1997
AFTER LIFE *after* Hirokazu Kore-eda
BUNNY
BURYING YOUR BROTHER IN
THE PAVEMENT
A CHRISTMAS CAROL *after* Dickens
THE END OF HISTORY…
HOPE
JACK THORNE PLAYS: ONE
JACK THORNE PLAYS: TWO
JUNKYARD
LET THE RIGHT ONE IN
after John Ajvide Lindqvist
THE MOTIVE AND THE CUE
MYDIDAE
THE SOLID LIFE OF SUGAR WATER
STACY & FANNY AND FAGGOT
WHEN YOU CURE ME
WHEN WINSTON WENT TO WAR WITH
THE WIRELESS
WOYZECK *after* Büchner

debbie tucker green
BORN BAD
DEBBIE TUCKER GREEN PLAYS: ONE
DIRTY BUTTERFLY
EAR FOR EYE
HANG
NUT
A PROFOUNDLY AFFECTIONATE,
PASSIONATE DEVOTION TO
SOMEONE (– *NOUN*)
RANDOM
STONING MARY
TRADE & GENERATIONS
TRUTH AND RECONCILIATION

David Haig

MAGIC

NICK HERN BOOKS
London
www.nickhernbooks.co.uk

A Nick Hern Book

Magic first published in Great Britain in 2026 as a paperback original by Nick Hern Books Limited, The Glasshouse, 49a Goldhawk Road, London W12 8QP

Cover image by Bob King Creative for Chichester Festival Theatre; photograph of David Haig as Conan Doyle and Hadley Fraser as Houdini by Seamus Ryan

Designed and typeset by Nick Hern Books, London
Printed in Great Britain by Mimco Ltd, Huntingdon, Cambridgeshire PE29 6XX

A CIP catalogue record for this book is available from the British Library

ISBN 978 1 83904 577 6

Woodland CARBON
www.woodlandcarbon.co.uk
NICK HERN BOOKS
Printed on Carbon Captured paper

www.nickhernbooks.co.uk/environmental-policy

Nick Hern Books' authorised representative in the EU is
Easy Access System Europe – Mustamäe tee 50, 10621 Tallinn, Estonia
email gpsr.requests@easproject.com

Magic was first produced by and performed at Chichester Festival Theatre on 24 April 2026, with the following cast (in alphabetical order):

BESS HOUDINI	Jenna Augen
HARRY HOUDINI	Hadley Fraser
ARTHUR CONAN DOYLE	David Haig
DR CRANDON	Ben Jones
JEAN CONAN DOYLE	Claire Price
TROUPE	Marc Serratosa
TROUPE	Ella Tekere
TROUPE	François Testory
MINA CRANDON	Jade Williams
TROUPE	Kristin Wei Wong
Director	Lucy Bailey
Designer	Joanna Parker
Lighting Designer	Aideen Malone
Illusion Designer	John Bulleid
Composer	Orlando Gough
Sound Designer	Beth Duke
Video Designer	Dick Straker
Movement Director	Ayse Tashkiran
Fight Director	Kate Waters
Casting Director	Ginny Schiller CDG
Voice & Dialect Coach	Edda Sharpe
Assistant Director	Joanna Pidcock
Dramaturg	Will Mortimer
Production Manager	Chris Boone
Costume Supervisor	Sian Harris
Hair, Wigs & Make-Up	Mark Marson for Campbell Young Associates
Props Supervisor	Jonathan Hall for Marcus Hall Props
Illusions Associate	Patrick Ashe
Company Stage Manager	Sally Hughes
Deputy Stage Manager	Rob Le Maistre
Assistant Stage Manager	Elsa Gear
Assistant Stage Manager	Krystal (Xinyu) Fan

Characters

HARRY HOUDINI
BESS HOUDINI
ARTHUR CONAN DOYLE
JEAN CONAN DOYLE
DR CRANDON
MINA CRANDON

And HECKLERS, STAGE MANAGER, ASSISTANTS

This text went to press before the end of rehearsals and so may differ slightly from the play as performed.

ACT ONE

Scene One

The Hippodrome Theatre. New York City. 1920.

A golden pool of light illuminates a rectangular hole in the stage.

A body slowly emerges through the hole.

HARRY HOUDINI *lies on his back, tightly buckled into a straitjacket. Still and expressionless, like a mummy. A heavy, rusted chain descends from the ceiling, stopping by his ankles.*

Mademoiselle Beatrice (HOUDINI*'s wife,* BESS) *struts on, dressed in performance sparkle. She attaches the chain to* HOUDINI*'s ankles. The chain ascends, winching* HOUDINI, *feet first, into the air.*

He twists and writhes, performing an inverted dance of death, as he begins his escape from the straitjacket. The image is macabre, he looks like a hanged man, albeit from his ankles not his neck.

Eventually, HOUDINI *has the jacket off, he hurls it into the audience. For a second he hangs motionless, arms outstretched, like Christ crucified upside down.* BESS *kneels below him, Mary Mother of Jesus praying for her son.*

A coffin rises through the rectangular hole in the stage.

The chain descends again. HOUDINI *is lowered into the coffin. He folds his arms over his chest like a corpse.* BESS *unclips the chain from his ankles and closes the lid on her husband. She holds up a hammer to the audience, then nails the lid shut. The bang of her hammer is percussive as she sings her signature tune:*

BESS.
Rosabelle, sweet Rosabelle
I love you more than I can tell.
O'er me you cast a spell,
I love you, my sweet Rosabelle.

She fastens the rusted chain to the coffin. The coffin rises into the air, high over the audience's head.

Suddenly there's an explosion and the coffin bursts apart. It swings vertically, the lid gaping open. The coffin is empty. HOUDINI *has disappeared.*

Another explosion. Gold stars and coloured smoke pour into the air. HOUDINI *steps out of the smoke, centre-stage, immaculately dressed in tails, starched white shirt, high collar and white bow tie.*

He flings his arms out wide. Powerful, exultant.

HOUDINI. I am Houdini!! The greatest mystifier since the dawn of creation!!

Blackout.

Scene Two

Houdini's dressing room. The only crucial details are a poster of Jack Dempsey, the Heavyweight Boxing Champion of the World, taped to his make-up mirror – signed by Dempsey himself. And a punchbag, ready for use, in the middle of the room.

HOUDINI *is on the move, still energised.* BESS, *on the other hand, sits quietly… rolling a joint.*

HOUDINI. You think he'll come?

BESS. Dunno, honey.

HOUDINI. Hope he does.

BESS. I hope so too. He's the bee's knees.

HOUDINI (*pointing at* BESS*'s joint*). No weed in the theatre, Bess.

BESS. Just rolling for later.

HOUDINI. Don't know why you need to do it.

BESS. You love my laugh, Harry.

HOUDINI. I do.

BESS. Dope makes me laugh.

HOUDINI. You laugh when you're not stoned.

BESS. Not as much as when I *am* stoned.

HOUDINI. You know what they say. Too much of a good thing. I may start to hate your laugh.

HOUDINI *goes to the door and looks out.*

BESS. No sign?

HOUDINI. No. He ain't coming.

HOUDINI *paces,* BESS *rolls.*

One of the hinges was stiff on the back panel. Any stiffer, I'd have had problems getting out.

BESS. I'll talk to Jim.

HOUDINI. You gonna make a note of it?

BESS. Sure.

HOUDINI. And the stitching on the bow tie.

BESS. To the collar?

HOUDINI. It's loose.

BESS. Okay.

HOUDINI *idly picks up a pack of cards. He shuffles – the shuffle is a thing of beauty.*

HOUDINI. I thought he would, Bess, I really thought he would.

He puts down the cards, goes to the punchbag and launches a series of punches.

Show me some respect, Sir Arthur, c'mon.

He punches the bag again.

We got stuff to talk about.

He skips, bobs and weaves. He boxes like a pro.

It's at this moment that SIR ARTHUR *and* LADY CONAN DOYLE *cross the stage and wait outside Houdini's dressing room.*

(CONAN DOYLE *is 6'3" and sports a walrus moustache. He exudes benign avuncularity.* LADY JEAN *is a handsome Home Counties wife. This first impression of the Doyles is almost completely inaccurate.*)

HOUDINI *continues to pound the punchbag.*

CONAN DOYLE. A man after my own heart!

BESS (*looking up, a large spliff in her mouth*). Oh hello.

HOUDINI *stops boxing and holds out his hand to* CONAN DOYLE, *a huge grin on his face.*

HOUDINI. Sir Arthur! Welcome to New York City!

CONAN DOYLE. What a magnificent performance, Mr Houdini.

HOUDINI. Just 'Houdini' please. Thank you so much for coming to my show.

CONAN DOYLE. I wouldn't have missed it for the world.

HOUDINI. It's a great honour to meet you. This is my wife, Bess. Bess, Sir Arthur Conan Doyle.

BESS. We think you're the cat's pyjamas, sir!

CONAN DOYLE. I'm flattered. (*Introducing* LADY JEAN.) This is my dear wife, Jean.

HOUDINI. How do you do.

BESS. What do I call you?

LADY JEAN. Call me?

BESS. Dame Jean? Lady Jean?

LADY JEAN. Just Jean.

BESS. Just Jean, okay.

LADY JEAN. Well… Jean.

BESS. I get ya.

HOUDINI. In my humble way, I think of myself as a writer… in the foothills, you know, and I look up at the peaks around me and there you are… Everest.

CONAN DOYLE (*a tiny smile*). Well…

HOUDINI. I have first editions of all the Sherlock Holmes stories in my library, well not *all*, I'm missing *A Study in Scarlet*, but two shelves dedicated to the great detective. I read them aloud to Bess.

BESS. *Hound of the Baskervilles* three times!

HOUDINI. Greatest story ever told. I truly believe that.

BESS. If I wasn't married to Harry, I'd wanna marry Dr Watson. He is cute.

LADY JEAN. We so enjoyed your performance.

CONAN DOYLE. You are a marvellous, extraordinary phenomenon. One day you must tell me how you manage such feats of dematerialisation.

HOUDINI (*enigmatic*). Well… it is what it is.

CONAN DOYLE. I've no doubt.

LADY JEAN. I am of course completely flummoxed. How did you do it?

HOUDINI (*faux-mystical*). With a little assistance from the other side.

LADY JEAN (*very serious*). My husband certainly thinks that's the case.

HOUDINI. He does?

HOUDINI *laughs,* CONAN DOYLE *doesn't.*

No, I'm afraid there's nothing magical about it, just a lot of hard work.

CONAN DOYLE *looks at* HOUDINI *steadily.*

CONAN DOYLE. I wonder.

CONAN DOYLE *smiles benignly and walks over to the punchbag.*

I have a punchbag in my 'writing room'. When the creative juices are a wee bit sluggish, I'll box for twenty minutes. It liberates the brain cells.

LADY JEAN. My worry is that it liberates them permanently.

CONAN DOYLE *taps the poster on Houdini's make-up mirror.*

CONAN DOYLE. The Manassa Mauler.

HOUDINI. Jack Dempsey.

CONAN DOYLE. Oh, I know who he is. I love all sports, but boxing transcends them all. It's a glorious thing, to see two pugilists after ten rounds, faces battered, lips bleeding, muscles like tree roots. It's brutal, yes, but there's a spiritual side too. To witness the limits of human endurance and courage is a lesson in itself.

HOUDINI. I agree with that. Go to the edge of the cliff and something special happens. I *really* agree with that.

CONAN DOYLE. I see the Mauler's signed your poster?

HOUDINI. Jack is my good friend. The greatest fighter in the history of the ring.

CONAN DOYLE (*a smile*). Carpentier's quicker. Tunney's more intelligent.

HOUDINI. They don't come close to Jack. People think he's just a street fighter, but I tell ya, he's a boxing scientist. He taught me how to deliver a punch with maximum power. Would you be interested in hearing what he told me?

CONAN DOYLE. I'd be fascinated.

HOUDINI (*making a decision*). Show me your guard.

CONAN DOYLE (*smiling*). I think we're going to rub along well, Houdini.

CONAN DOYLE *takes guard. It's a powerful but old-fashioned boxing stance – head back, right arm extended.*

HOUDINI. Terrific!

BESS *pulls over a chair for* LADY JEAN.

BESS. Why don't you sit down, Jean, the boys are gonna be in the playground for a while.

HOUDINI (*examining* CONAN DOYLE*'s guard*). You left-handed?

CONAN DOYLE (*raising his left fist in the air*). Southpaw!

HOUDINI. Who's your favourite lefty?

CONAN DOYLE. Tiger Flowers every time.

HOUDINI. I love Tiger! Great fighter, good friend of mine.

CONAN DOYLE (*dropping his guard for a moment*). I saw him fight Billy Hooper at the Auditorium in Atlanta, Georgia.

HOUDINI. You did? I am a jealous man.

CONAN DOYLE. What a fight! He carried a Bible into the ring.

HOUDINI. Oh sure, Tiger is a devoutly religious guy. Show me your guard again.

CONAN DOYLE *does so.*

Okay, so this is a classic nineteenth-century guard.

CONAN DOYLE. Not surprising, I learned to box in the eighties.

HOUDINI. I ain't criticising, I love it, very side-on, extended lead hand, it's a fine guard. Hit the bag, Sir Arthur.

CONAN DOYLE *removes his jacket and hands it to* LADY JEAN.

CONAN DOYLE. This is not how I thought the evening would end.

HOUDINI. Hit the bag with a straight left.

CONAN DOYLE *lands a slightly rigid but extremely powerful blow. The bag flies backwards.* BESS *applauds wildly.*

BESS. On the button! That punchbag ain't gonna get up! (*To* LADY JEAN.) Where d'you two live?

LADY JEAN. Crowborough.

BESS. The Cobra from Crowborough!

LADY JEAN (*clapping her hands*). The King of Crowborough!

BESS. Beautiful, Jean! The King of Crowborough!

CONAN DOYLE *lands another powerful blow.*

The Crowborough Killer!

LADY JEAN. The Crowborough Killer!

HOUDINI. Okay, this is what my friend Jack Dempsey told me. You start the punch with your hand half open, and just inches from your target you suddenly close the hand with a… convulsive SNAP! So when the fist smashes into the bag, it will be steel-hard from the sudden grabbing tension. You got me?

CONAN DOYLE. I think so.

BESS (*enjoying herself*). This is just the elephant's eyebrows!

HOUDINI. Most boxers clench their fist before they launch the punch. That true with you?

CONAN DOYLE. I clench my fist and then I punch.

HOUDINI. So all the energy in your arm is dissipated. Don't clench until your fist is inches from your target. That's how Dempsey generates his power.

CONAN DOYLE *lands two incredibly powerful blows on the punchbag.*

Yeah!

HOUDINI *pulls* CONAN DOYLE *round to face him.*

Now imagine we're fighting – you're Willard, six-six, weighing two forty-five…

CONAN DOYLE. That would be useful.

HOUDINI. …and I'm Dempsey, five-nine, weighing a hundred and eighty. I gotta make every punch count.

They circle each other. The heavyweight and the bantamweight, mismatched but lithe and professional.

LADY JEAN. This will definitely end badly.

BESS. I love it!

HOUDINI. I'm crouching and I do the shoulder whirl, like turning handlebars on a bicycle, left right, left right, I come under your defence, I hit you with a straight right.

HOUDINI *places his right hand on* CONAN DOYLE*'s chin.* CONAN DOYLE *retreats and raises his guard.* HOUDINI *attacks again.*

I never stop moving. Crouching, bobbing, weaving, and I come under again, whirling handlebars, this time I hook.

But CONAN DOYLE *deflects the blow and jabs with his right. He makes contact and hits* HOUDINI *a little too hard, flush on the chin.* HOUDINI *is shocked and jumps back. A silence. They stare at each other, then:*

Goddamn… Touché…

The atmosphere has changed. LADY JEAN *and* BESS *stand.* HOUDINI *and* CONAN DOYLE *circle again.*

CONAN DOYLE. Now I come at you, Houdini.

CONAN DOYLE *closes in. An exchange of blows, genuine punches, hitting flesh. The two men realise they are actually fighting.*

Intense concentration on their faces. CONAN DOYLE *is now gasping for breath and dripping with sweat.*

LADY JEAN. Arthur…

HOUDINI *is fit as a fiddle, he moves in again, but* CONAN DOYLE *is ready for him. With his superior reach, he lands a punch in* HOUDINI*'s stomach.*

HOUDINI. You can hit me there all day, don't feel a thing.

HOUDINI *advances again, ruthless this time, he crouches under* CONAN DOYLE*'s defence and lands an uppercut to* CONAN DOYLE*'s stomach.* CONAN DOYLE *is instantly* *winded and drops his guard. Red-faced and exhausted, he struggles to breathe.* LADY JEAN *tries to get to him.*

LADY JEAN. Arthur!

BESS. Enough, boys!

CONAN DOYLE *collapses onto* HOUDINI. *Arms round his neck. Their faces are close.* HOUDINI *starts laughing.* CONAN DOYLE *is gasping, but now giggling like a schoolboy.* HOUDINI *laughs helplessly, he pats* CONAN DOYLE*'s head.*

HOUDINI. Hey, you're good!

CONAN DOYLE. You're 'no' bad yersel''.

HOUDINI. Oh boy! Boxing with my hero!

BESS. You only met ten minutes ago.

CONAN DOYLE. And now we're friends.

HOUDINI. Good friends.

The two prizefighters lean on each other – CONAN DOYLE, *so happy but still struggling to breathe.*

CONAN DOYLE. I can't breathe! I literally can't breathe!

LADY JEAN. Very foolish.

CONAN DOYLE. Fun though.

HOUDINI *leads* CONAN DOYLE *to a chair. He lowers his massive frame and sits.* HOUDINI *sits beside him.*

CONAN DOYLE *loops an arm round* HOUDINI*'s shoulder. His chest is still heaving but he's happy. The two men continue to laugh, like boys sharing a private joke.*

LADY JEAN. Loosen your tie, Arthur.

CONAN DOYLE *does what he's told.*

Undo your top button.

He obeys. The two men are comfortable in each other's presence, as if they've known each other for years.

CONAN DOYLE. Thank you for your letter.

HOUDINI. You're welcome.

CONAN DOYLE. And for the book.

BESS. Did you send him the new one, honey?

HOUDINI. Nothing to do with my writing.

BESS. Harry's writing a crime story, but he's kinda stuck. He wants to ask your advice.

CONAN DOYLE. Your husband sent me a history of spiritualism.

HOUDINI. It's your subject, Sir Arthur.

CONAN DOYLE. It is. (*A beat.*) Is it yours too?

Silence. They seem to be sizing each other up.

What interests me, Houdini, is that not only do you have two shelves in your library dedicated to Sherlock Holmes, but I understand you also have the biggest private collection of spiritualist literature in the world. Over two thousand written records of séances held since 1848.

HOUDINI. Hey, you did your research!

CONAN DOYLE. Am I correct?

HOUDINI. You are. Would you like to see the collection?

CONAN DOYLE. You *know* I would!!

HOUDINI. You'd be very welcome. Bess and I would love to entertain you at Houdini House, while you're on this side of the puddle.

CONAN DOYLE. That would be wonderful! Thank you.

BESS. Oh yeah! What a swell idea!

HOUDINI. I got a lot to show ya!

CONAN DOYLE. I can't think of anything more exciting! (*Slumping back in his chair.*) My goodness, I am absolutely exhausted.

HOUDINI. We need to get you in shape.

CONAN DOYLE. Too late. Old and creaky.

LADY JEAN. One of these days your heart will just stop.

CONAN DOYLE. Well, if it does, it does. I expect boxing to be a priority in the spirit world, so keeping in trim is an investment.

CONAN DOYLE *clasps* HOUDINI*'s hand.*

This has been… a wee bit spiritual, don't you think?

HOUDINI. Edge of the cliff, Sir Arthur!

They smile at each other. HOUDINI *suddenly lifts* CONAN DOYLE*'s hand into the air, like a boxer at the end of a bout.*

Edge of the goddamn cliff!!

Blackout.

Scene Three

Houdini's library at 278, W.113th St, Harlem. Houdini memorabilia everywhere, two rows of old theatre seats provide seating.

CONAN DOYLE *is awestruck. He stands in front of a 'wall' of books and documents.* HOUDINI *watches as* CONAN DOYLE *gently examines some of the volumes.*

CONAN DOYLE. Frederick Hockley, Alfred Wallace – (*Taking down a book.*) *Natural Magic* first edition, 1658! This is extraordinary! (*Selecting another book.*) *Mina Crandon the Medium* by Malcolm Bird. Have you met Mrs Crandon?

HOUDINI. I always wanted to.

CONAN DOYLE. She is the finest medium I've ever sat with. I'd love you to meet her.

He replaces the book.

(*A third book.*) Oh my goodness, *The Discoverie of Witchcraft*, first edition again, 1584!

HOUDINI. Not bad, huh?

CONAN DOYLE. Absolutely extraordinary. How long has it taken?

HOUDINI. Over ten years.

CONAN DOYLE. I'm not surprised.

HOUDINI. I'm a new aspirant in the world of literature, Arthur, but I'm proud of this. It's the climax of my studies and labours.

CONAN DOYLE. You should be *very* proud.

CONAN DOYLE *moves his hand reverently along a line of books then turns to* HOUDINI.

Why? (*Silence.*) Why, Houdini?

HOUDINI. I seek the truth.

CONAN DOYLE. So do I.

HOUDINI. The *truth*, Sir Arthur.

CONAN DOYLE. We could search together.

HOUDINI. Sounds good to me.

CONAN DOYLE. I have abandoned writing. Fiction at least. Friend and foe pester me to give them more of the monstrous growth that is Sherlock Holmes, but I resist.

HOUDINI. No more Holmes?

CONAN DOYLE. Not if I can help it.

HOUDINI. Gosh, that's sad.

CONAN DOYLE. Not sad at all! My sole remaining purpose in life is to spread the word about spiritualism, which I believe is the most important religious development since the birth of Jesus Christ.

HOUDINI. I agree… if it's true.

They are interrupted by BESS *and* LADY JEAN *entering.* BESS *carries a tray of four opened bottles of Coca-Cola.*

BESS. Four Coca-Colas! I've added a little something to two of them, a small dose of harbour gin.

HOUDINI. Illegally distilled in our neighbour's backyard.

BESS. Gin and Coke for you, Jean…

LADY JEAN. Thank you very much.

BESS. Gin and Coke for me! Frankly, I think it's kooky that the women are the boozehounds here and the men are the teetotallers. But that's your funeral, boys!

She hands round the drinks.

I would've got ya rum, Jean, but even on Harry's fees, it's outta reach. Cheers!

They clink bottles.

Here's to the end of prohibition!

They take a glug of Coke. LADY JEAN *is instantly poleaxed. She tries to breathe normally.*

LADY JEAN. Oh dear!… Aaah… that is… quite a taste!

BESS. I know, it's rotgut. I can't wait to get to London next summer! I wanna taste the real McCoy again, some decent giggle juice, for God's sake! (*Changing the subject.*) Hey, Arthur, did Harry tell you, the top two shelves are the 'Sherlock Shelves'?

CONAN DOYLE. He did.

BESS. You see the gap, top shelf on the left?

CONAN DOYLE. I do.

BESS. That's where we're gonna slot in our first edition of *A Study in Scarlet*, if we find one.

HOUDINI. Which we will, honey, we will hunt one down.

CONAN DOYLE. It was the original Holmes story, so first editions are hard to come by.

BESS (*as if to an idiot*). I know it's the original story, Arthur! *Study in Scarlet* is my second favourite after *Hound of the*

Baskervilles. I practically can recite the book by heart. I do Holmes and Watson's first meeting as a party piece.

LADY JEAN. I'd like to hear that.

CONAN DOYLE. So would I.

BESS. 'Dr Watson, this is Mr Sherlock Holmes.' 'How are ya?' said Holmes cordially, gripping Watson's hand with surprising strength. 'You have been in Afghanistan, I perceive.' 'Hot dog! How did you know?' Watson asked in astonishment.

CONAN DOYLE. Brilliant! One or two words I didn't recognise.

BESS. Oh yeah, I had to change it a little, I play to New Yorkers.

LADY JEAN. Understandable. (*Taking a sip of Coke.*) The second sip is slightly easier.

BESS. Always, honey.

HOUDINI. So everything below the Sherlock Shelves is dedicated to spiritualism. The bottom shelf is just séances. Over two thousand. Starting on the left – (*Removing a thin document.*) a handwritten description of the first ever recorded séance in November 1848.

He replaces the document.

The shelf is chronological and ends here on the right – (*Pulling out another document.*) with a séance held only last Tuesday at the Jewish Spiritualist Society on West Eighty-Fourth and Broadway.

CONAN DOYLE. May I see?

HOUDINI *hands* CONAN DOYLE *the record of the Tuesday séance*. CONAN DOYLE *flicks through the document as he speaks*.

Did you attend this séance?

HOUDINI. I did.

CONAN DOYLE. And?

HOUDINI. For me, nothing. As per usual.

CONAN DOYLE (*falling silent as he reads one particular entry*). Aaaah, this is very touching. A mother, Amy Fairchild, contacted the spirit of her dead son, killed in action at the Battle of the Marne. A huge number of American casualties in that battle.

LADY JEAN. It sounds very familiar.

BESS. Did you lose family in the war, Arthur?

CONAN DOYLE (*very simply*). My son Kingsley was shot through the throat on the first day of the Battle of the Somme.

BESS. Oh gosh.

CONAN DOYLE. No, no! No sympathy please, I'm merely stating facts. My brother Innes died of Spanish flu, Jean's brother Malcolm, was shot dead on the retreat from Mons, my nephew Oscar was blown up at Ypres. My brothers-in-law Lesley and Alec died from their wounds.

HOUDINI. You've paid your price.

CONAN DOYLE. Honestly, I don't seek sympathy. There are many families in the same situation. My point is that spiritualism brings solace to a tortured world.

BESS (*guileless*). You mean it ain't true, but if it's what folks need – it don't do no harm.

CONAN DOYLE (*calm and factual*). I don't... *think* that the spirits of the dead contact the living. I *KNOW* they do. Things I have seen, heard, touched, leave *no* room for doubt. Not wishful thinking, Bess, but a concrete reassurance that all those fine fellows, those splendid... boys... my son Kingsley included, did not simply dissipate into nothing.

He smiles.

No. In fact they're all thoroughly enjoying a better life now.

BESS. Good for them!

CONAN DOYLE. I hope to be in touch with Kingsley soon, I haven't as yet made contact.

LADY JEAN (*simple, sincere*). But I have.

BESS (*resisting a smile*). You spoke to your dead son?

LADY JEAN. He spoke to me. Or rather he channelled his thoughts through me and I wrote them down. You look surprised.

BESS. You're right, I wasn't expecting you to say that.

LADY JEAN. I was certainly surprised! We were on holiday in Cornwall with my dear friend Lily, who is a very powerful medium, and I was literally spreading clotted cream on a scone, when I felt the strangest tingling in my fingers. Lily put down her cup of tea and asked me: 'Are you feeling the urge to write?' You could have knocked me down with a feather, I said: 'Yes, yes I am.' It turns out that I have a particular psychic gift. Spirits communicate through my hand and I am able to write down their thoughts and feelings. You can imagine I was bowled over. As you can see, I'm a very ordinary housewife.

CONAN DOYLE. You are *never* ordinary, darling.

LADY JEAN. Oh I am. I'm not ashamed of the fact. As I always say, a clever man should never marry a woman of equal intelligence.

CONAN DOYLE. I should never have married you then, should I?

LADY JEAN. Anyway Kingsley has been in touch. He wanted to assure Arthur that he will make contact soon. We're very excited.

BESS. Well I wish Harry's mom would get in touch with you, Jean, he misses her terrible. Don't you, sweetheart?

HOUDINI *is silent, unable to respond.*

Harry?

Still no response.

You miss her every day, don't you, honey?

HOUDINI. She was an angel upon earth.

BESS. She was the cat's meow. Bess Houdini always came second.

LADY JEAN. Oh I know the feeling, Mrs Houdini! Arthur idolised his mother.

CONAN DOYLE. For good reason.

HOUDINI. 'Beatrice Beautiful', you were never number two. I loved you both equally. My two sweethearts.

CONAN DOYLE. When did your mother pass over?

HOUDINI. Six years, eleven months and three days ago.

BESS. Nearly seven years, but only yesterday Harry says to me: 'I do not think I will recover.' No kidding. 'I do not think I will ever recover from Mama's passing.'

HOUDINI. What if I don't want to recover?

CONAN DOYLE (*heartfelt*). I know that feeling. My mother died earlier this year.

BESS. You've had a tough time, Arthur.

CONAN DOYLE. She was the helmsman.

BESS. Same with you, Harry. Without Cecilia, you woulda crash-landed.

CONAN DOYLE *pats* HOUDINI*'s knee*.

CONAN DOYLE. We're two of a kind. Have you tried to communicate with your mother since she passed over?

Silence.

Houdini?

CONAN DOYLE *and* LADY JEAN *wait for* HOUDINI*'s response*. *Eventually:*

HOUDINI. I have been to hundreds, no kidding, *hundreds* of séances since my sainted mother passed… hoping… *longing*… I wanted it to be true, I still do… But nothing. Not once.

Short silence.

CONAN DOYLE. I have a proposal. When you're next performing in the United Kingdom, I'd like to invite you both to Windlesham Manor, and if Mina Crandon is still in the country, she's touring England at the moment, I'm determined to introduce you.

BESS. The medium? Oh boy, that'll please Harry, I hear she's a sheba!

CONAN DOYLE. I don't know what a sheba is, Bess, but as a medium… she has an extraordinary presence.

HOUDINI. Prove that the dead speak to the living and I'm your devoted disciple, but you have to prove it to me. Conclusively. Scientifically.

CONAN DOYLE. My degree was in medicine, physics was at the centre of my education. I have no interest in a religion which isn't based on scientific truth. But I have a wee secret, I have actually seen your show five times since we arrived in New York.

HOUDINI. I'm flattered. You should've told me.

CONAN DOYLE. And I am increasingly convinced that you are not entirely straightforward with your public. You claim you are merely a performer…

HOUDINI. Never 'merely'. (*Factual.*) I am the greatest illusionist this world has ever known.

CONAN DOYLE. Oh my goodness, I agree with that, but ultimately you claim that what you do is artifice. But I suspect… you have a dematerialising and reconstructing force that can momentarily separate the molecules of a solid object. My background as a physicist, tells me you have this wonderful power.

A very long silence. HOUDINI *and* CONAN DOYLE *stare into each other's eyes.*

HOUDINI. I do not.

Another silence.

CONAN DOYLE. Sit with Mrs Crandon, and if you are persuaded… join our cause. Add your voice to mine. You and I would be a force to be reckoned with.

Blackout.

Scene Four

Months later. A Victorian theatre in London. Packed audience.

Centre-stage: a very ornate, circular bar table. Upstage: a huge board displaying a stencil of four mathematical equations.

CONAN DOYLE, *dressed in white tie and tails, addresses the audience.*

CONAN DOYLE. Ladies and gentlemen, would you welcome to the stage, for the last time tonight, my assistant – Lady Jean Doyle.

LADY JEAN *enters, wearing a Pre-Raphaelite evening dress. She trails a richly coloured train. In her outstretched hands she carries a blood-red velvet cushion. On the cushion sit two tuning forks and a shining brass ball.* LADY JEAN*'s expression is profoundly solemn.*

She places the cushion on the bar table. CONAN DOYLE *and* LADY JEAN *each select a tuning fork and hold it aloft.*

What we are about to show you requires absolute silence.

The audience quietens.

Thank you.

CONAN DOYLE *picks up the brass ball. He strikes the fork on the ball.*

I strike a tuning fork.

The sound is picked up by ambient microphoning, producing a sublimely pure and ethereal note which fills the auditorium.

My assistant holds a second fork, she doesn't strike it, and yet it starts to vibrate and emit the same note as the first. Sympathetic resonance. (*Striking the fork again.*) A disturbance of sound waves has travelled at one thousand, one hundred and twenty-five feet per second, from one fork to the other. Magical physics!

CONAN DOYLE *turns upstage to the giant stencil of equations.*

Now. Maxwell's magnificent, mystical equations. They prove that light is an electromagnetic wave that travels at one hundred and eighty-six thousand miles… per second!

A powerful shaft of light bursts through the cut-out shapes of the equations and the formulae dance on the faces of the audience and the walls of the theatre.

Now, if sound and light can hurtle through space, then why shouldn't the energy of thought? The physicist, Bernard Kazhinsky, believes that the brain releases electromagnetic waves when we think. 'Thought waves' in other words. And like sound and light, these thought waves travel at huge speed. So if our thoughts, feelings and emotions can travel and exist independently of the body, then it's logical to assume they're not trapped after death, our personalities survive. And I feel confident that as we learn more and more about electromagnetism, that contacting the spirits of the dead will eventually be as easy as writing a letter. Maybe not in our lifetimes, but it *will* happen. Contact with our grandparents, our mothers and fathers, brothers, sisters, friends… our sons and our daughters… to see them again, as vibrantly alive after death, as they were when we saw them last on the earth plane. Thank you for listening.

CONAN DOYLE *takes* LADY JEAN*'s hand. He bows and* LADY JEAN *drops into a deep curtsy.*

Blackout.

Lights up.

The show is over. CONAN DOYLE *and* LADY JEAN *are packing the tuning forks into a box. A* STAGE MANAGER *ushers* HOUDINI *and* BESS *onstage from the wings.*

HOUDINI. My turn to congratulate *you*!

CONAN DOYLE. Aaah, my dear sparring partner!

They embrace.

Wonderful to see you! Thank you for coming.

HOUDINI. Wouldn't have missed it for the world. Lady Jean.

LADY JEAN. Lovely to see you both.

CONAN DOYLE. Hello, Bess.

HOUDINI. What a performance!

BESS. You're a hell of an actor, Arthur!

CONAN DOYLE *(turning to* LADY JEAN). I don't think I was acting, was I?

HOUDINI. You were pretty damn convincing to me.

CONAN DOYLE. Well yes, I certainly believe what I said.

HOUDINI. Sure, but you gotta communicate that to your audience, an' I'm telling ya, your audience was one thousand per cent in your corner.

BESS. We all believed ya.

CONAN DOYLE. Good! Jean, do we have that…?

LADY JEAN. Oh yes, one moment…

LADY JEAN *leaves the stage.*

CONAN DOYLE. How's the Palladium?

HOUDINI. We love it!

CONAN DOYLE. You're the talk of the town.

BESS. I know, we're so swelled over it.

HOUDINI. We're setting London agog, Arthur! I wear my ice-cream suit, Bess wears her finest sparkle and the magic is taking flight.

CONAN DOYLE. I hear it's brilliant.

HOUDINI. So says the whole world except your *Daily Mirror.* The *Daily Mirror* says I talk too much about myself in a desperate attempt to be popular. They say I resemble a failed 'end-of-the-pier' magician. I tell ya, that penetrated my defences.

CONAN DOYLE. Entirely your fault for reading the *Mirror*.

HOUDINI. You only remember the bad reviews.

CONAN DOYLE. Are the houses good?

HOUDINI. Packed.

LADY JEAN (*returning from the wings*). Here we are.

She hands a 'book-shaped' parcel to CONAN DOYLE. CONAN DOYLE *presents it to* HOUDINI.

CONAN DOYLE. A little something to welcome you to England.

HOUDINI. Not necessary, but thank you. Shall I open it now?

CONAN DOYLE. Why not?

HOUDINI *unwraps the parcel*. CONAN DOYLE, BESS *and* LADY JEAN *watch intently. The wrapping paper is off, revealing a book*. HOUDINI *is completely overwhelmed*.

HOUDINI. Oy! Vos far a naches! Ikh kvell! (*Yiddish: 'What a joy, I'm so happy!'*) Thank you so much, Arthur.

CONAN DOYLE. Not at all.

HOUDINI *turns the pages gently, treating the book with the utmost awe and respect*.

HOUDINI. I… I'm speechless.

BESS. Which is rare. What's the book, Harry?

HOUDINI. It's a first edition of *A Study in Scarlet*.

BESS (*moved*). Oh baby!

HOUDINI. The only one we're missing. Jean, I have circled the globe, no exaggeration, looking for this edition. I have used my celebrity with no shame, trying to get a hold of it. But nowhere, nowhen.

BESS. That is the elephant's eyebrows, sweetheart.

HOUDINI. Oh yeah! Elephant's eyebrows.

HOUDINI *is reading an inscription at the front of the book*.

BESS. What's it say, honey?

HOUDINI. 'To complete your collection, from your sparring partner, the most celebrated southpaw in Sussex. Arthur "The Tiger" Conan Doyle.' (*Almost unable to speak.*) Oh gee. I will treasure this until I die.

CONAN DOYLE (*slight smile*). And afterwards perhaps.

HOUDINI. You think they read Sherlock Holmes on the other side?

CONAN DOYLE. I imagine literary taste is the same on both sides of the veil, so I don't see why not. (*A beat.*) The Crandons are looking forward to meeting you.

HOUDINI. It's mutual.

BESS. I'm kinda jumpy.

CONAN DOYLE. Why?

BESS. Ain't never been to a séance. Harry goes all the time, but I never went to one.

LADY JEAN. Oh they're not frightening at all.

BESS. No?

LADY JEAN. Quite the reverse, they're rather comforting.

BESS. Okay, I'm sitting next to you, Jean.

CONAN DOYLE. Well you couldn't have chosen a better one to start you off, Mina Crandon is the elephant's eyebrows.

Blackout.

Scene Five

Windlesham Manor, the Conan Doyles' home in Crowborough, Sussex.

CONAN DOYLE, HOUDINI, BESS *and* LADY JEAN *sit at a round table. On the table: pads and pencils, a lamp and a curious wooden box.*

BESS. You think we'll see spirits?

LADY JEAN. One can't guarantee it.

BESS. Kinda hope we don't.

CONAN DOYLE. It's not a performance, they don't appear on cue.

BESS. Your kids go to séances, Arthur?

CONAN DOYLE. We have a family séance once a day.

BESS. No!

HOUDINI. Are you serious?

LADY JEAN. Why's that peculiar?

CONAN DOYLE. You wouldn't question a Christian taking their family to church, would you?

BESS. That is *so* different.

CONAN DOYLE. It certainly isn't.

LADY JEAN. We're celebrating our faith with our children.

BESS. Jeez! That would scare the hell out of me. Don't want no ghosts following me round, tapping me on the shoulder in the middle of the night. I'm happy to wait 'n' see. When I die I'll know. Or I won't know, which is also fine.

CONAN DOYLE. You know we have nearly three thousand spiritualist churches now in the United Kingdom, over a million registered, practising spiritualists, we're growing by the day, but what our movement needs is a popular voice.

HOUDINI (*immediately bridling*). What do you mean 'popular'?

CONAN DOYLE. Well…

HOUDINI. I'm not a dime-show entertainer.

CONAN DOYLE. No.

HOUDINI. I'm not an end-of-the-pier magician.

CONAN DOYLE. Of course not.

HOUDINI. My audience is no different to yours. I've played to kings and queens.

BESS (*gentle*). We know that, honey.

HOUDINI. I played to Tsar Nicholas and Alexandra, I played to Rasputin, to Charlie Chaplin and Buster Keaton. Jack Dempsey, Theodore Roosevelt, Babe Ruth – they're my friends.

CONAN DOYLE. Which is exactly my point, you've played to everyone. The world listens to you.

BESS. You touched a nerve, Arthur.

HOUDINI (*furious*). I've written four books!

CONAN DOYLE. Yes.

HOUDINI. Have you read them?

CONAN DOYLE. I'm afraid I haven't.

HOUDINI. You should, I'd appreciate it if you could take a look at them, they're good. My voice is not 'popular', it is universal. I haven't studied grammar but I have studied locks and handcuffs as studiously as you read medicine. I am one of a kind, like Galileo, Alexander the Great, or Christopher Columbus. You can't define the Great Houdini, he's an artist, he's a mechanic, he's a man of letters…

HOUDINI *would continue, but he is interrupted by the entrance of* DR *and* MINA CRANDON. DR CRANDON (*an urbane Bostonian*) *leads his wife* MINA *to the table. She is beautiful. No make-up, hair down, she's wearing a black silk kimono. Her legs and feet are bare.*

MINA *is serious and focused, apparently unaware of the effect she is having. The effect is this: it's as if Marilyn Monroe had removed the outer trappings of her beauty and offered herself to the room – vulnerable, naked, seeking protection.*

BESS (*murmured*). Gosh. Oh my!

CONAN DOYLE *and* LADY JEAN *are transfixed.*

With embarrassed humility, MINA *lifts her arms and drops her head.*

DR CRANDON. Mina asks you to confirm she carries nothing on her person. It is such a sceptical world. (*Short silence.*) Gentlemen? Lady Jean? Please, no shame, no embarrassment.

CONAN DOYLE *and* LADY JEAN *step forward and shyly 'frisk'* MINA. *Their search is not comprehensive, they're aware of naked flesh under the kimono.*

Houdini?

HOUDINI. I trust you.

DR CRANDON. I would appreciate it, Houdini. You of all people.

Reluctantly, HOUDINI *frisks* MINA, *patting her body and legs. He eyeballs her.*

HOUDINI. Facts, Mrs Crandon, not apple sauce.

DR CRANDON *gently sits* MINA *down. The expression on her face is quite neutral, unaffected – no melodrama.*

BESS. Mrs Crandon?

No reply.

DR CRANDON. Mina is listening to you.

BESS. Will you keep your eye open for Harry's mom?

HOUDINI. Bess…

BESS. Don't worry, honey, I ain't gonna embarrass you. She died six years ago, Mrs Crandon, Harry would love to know if she's okay.

HOUDINI. Bess…

BESS. Only if you bump into her. No pressure.

DR CRANDON. Mina hears you, Mrs Houdini. We will conduct the sitting in red light.

He switches on the lamp which has a deep red bulb. He places it near MINA. *He then places the enigmatic wooden box in the middle of the table – out of* MINA*'s reach.*

This is the 'bellbox'.

He depresses a wooden flap on top of the box. A bell rings.

If Mina's spirit guide, Walter, comes through, he will ring the bell to announce his presence. The bell is out of Mina's reach, we live in a cynical world. Walter was my wife's brother. He passed over nine years ago. He eschewed the silver spoon and worked as a mechanic for the New Haven Railroad. He was crushed to death by a derailed train. There has always been much love between brother and sister. (*As an afterthought.*) Oh one other thing, a medium's feet are often a source of deception. Mina, why don't you rest your feet on Houdini's leg?

MINA *lifts her feet and places them in* HOUDINI*'s lap. Her expression is soft, a little lost.* HOUDINI*'s face: impassive.*

I'm going to turn off the lights now.

DR CRANDON *turns out the lights. The red lamp shines spectrally on* MINA*'s face. Her skin is rendered translucent, she looks dead.*

BESS. Jeepers creepers!

CONAN DOYLE. I think we should pray.

DR CRANDON. By all means.

CONAN DOYLE. Oh God, open our minds to receive guidance from the spirit world…

MINA *starts to sway gently, back and forth.*

Help us to connect with departed loved ones who wish to contact us on the earth plane…

As the prayer continues, one of MINA*'s hands strays up to her face, investigating a presence near her cheek. She brushes it away. Her other hand follows suit, both hands now pick at something invisible on her face. She tries to rub the presence off her skin.*

Help us to give and receive love…

Someone or something invisible tries to climb into MINA*'s head. Her movements become more frantic. She pushes the possessor away with all her might. She barks unintelligible words, the possessor responds: 'Let me, let me, l-l-l-let m-me.' The séance table starts lifting and falling, crashing violently. The battle continues, but then, succumbing to the inevitable,* MINA *stops fighting and welcomes in the spirit. Serenity returns to her face and the table settles again.*

Make us instruments of peace. If there is discord, help us to unite, where there is despair, give us hope.

Suddenly the red lamp goes out. Total, profound blackout. The dark silence stretches for fifteen, twenty, twenty-five seconds. Then with no warning a white ball of psychic light whizzes off the séance table and fires into the audience. It explodes, loudly, into blinding white light, illuminating, for a second, hundreds of faces.

BESS. Fuck! Oh my God!

Darkness again, then a second ball of light shoots out of the auditorium and this time explodes dazzlingly over the heads of the actors.

(*Very scared.*) Shit!

Darkness again. The sound of a gale-force wind screams through the theatre. Freezing air rushes through the auditorium. Then just as suddenly, the wind drops.

Silence returns. Into this silence, the bellbox on the séance table rings. Three times – a clean, pure sound. Followed by a long, piercing whistle.

The red lamp switches on again, lighting up MINA*'s face. Her expression is no longer serene. Her mouth is distorted, her eyes are screwed up.* WALTER*, her dead brother, her spirit guide, speaks through her. A guttural, deep bark of a voice comes from the pit of* MINA*'s stomach.*

WALTER. Hi, little sis! I'm here. Happy birthday for next Thursday. Here's a little something in advance.

A bunch of luminous flowers falls out of the darkness and lands with a bang on the séance table.

White roses. Your favourites.

MINA (*her own gentle voice, but distant, slightly slurred*). Thank you, Walter.

WALTER. Why's the magician here? Is he here to cause trouble?

MINA. No, I'm sure he's not.

WALTER. Hey, Houdini, are you honourable? Houdini, I asked you a question. Are you honourable?

HOUDINI. I am. Are you?

WALTER. I don't trust him, Mina.

MINA. He's here as Sir Arthur's friend.

WALTER. Maybe, maybe not. Sweetheart, I miss you, do you miss me?

MINA. Always.

WALTER. It's beautiful over here. You should come soon.

MINA. I long to. But I'm only thirty-two.

WALTER. Thirty-three.

MINA. Not till Thursday.

There is ambient microphoning around the stage. WALTER*'s voice moves from speaker to speaker as if he's walking round the room.*

WALTER. Little sis?… I have…

MINA. What is it?

WALTER. I have someone with me, he's been on this side a while now… He's desperate to come through… I said I'd help if I could.

MINA. Is it a man or a woman?

WALTER. It's a young man… A kid really.

MINA. Is he with you now?

WALTER. He's here. He knows someone at the table… an older man… hey, kid, is it your pa you wanna talk to?

MINA. What's his name, Walter?

WALTER. What's your name, kid? I can't quite… is it?… Kin… King…

CONAN DOYLE (*profoundly moved*). Kingsley.

WALTER. Kid, is your name Kingsley?

CONAN DOYLE. Dear boy, is it you? Speak to me if you can. It's your father. I'm here.

Silence.

Kingsley, speak to me. Speak to me.

KINGSLEY. Here I am, Father. It is I. I am speaking through Mrs Crandon, but I am here.

CONAN DOYLE. Dear boy… are you… are you well?

KINGSLEY. I am.

CONAN DOYLE. Are you happy?

KINGSLEY. I'm happy *now*.

CONAN DOYLE. Not in pain?

KINGSLEY. There is no pain on the other side. And, Father, this will amuse you, the mole on my ankle has disappeared completely! Oscar and Malcolm send their love to you.

CONAN DOYLE. Thank you.

KINGSLEY. I have tried so often to come through. To talk to you. To tell you I'm well.

CONAN DOYLE. This is so… joyful. Can I touch you?

KINGSLEY. I don't think so.

CONAN DOYLE. But you *are* here with me?

KINGSLEY. I am.

CONAN DOYLE. Your stepmother is here.

No response.

Kingsley, your stepmother Jean is here.

KINGSLEY. Hello Mama.

LADY JEAN. Hello Kingsley.

KINGSLEY. Father… forgive me.

CONAN DOYLE. Forgive what?

KINGSLEY. Forgive me for not believing in the spirit world.

CONAN DOYLE. There's nothing to forgive.

KINGSLEY. It exists and it is a happy place… a happy… happy… (*Getting fainter.*) happy place.

Silence.

CONAN DOYLE. Are you there, dear boy? Are you there?

WALTER. The boy's gone, sis. I gotta scoot too. Happy trails, sweetheart, happy birthday…

There is a loud crash as the screens behind MINA *fall backwards and hit the floor. For a few seconds, the violent gale returns.*

Then sudden, total silence.

MINA *licks her parched lips and moans slightly as she comes out of trance.* DR CRANDON *switches on the lights. Cruel, white light.* MINA*'s kimono is dishevelled, she looks utterly spent.*

CONAN DOYLE *is hunched over the table, shuddering with emotion, tears rolling down his cheeks.* LADY JEAN *hurries over to him.*

LADY JEAN. I'm here, Arthur. I'm here.

CONAN DOYLE (*smiling through his tears*). Did you hear him?

LADY JEAN. Yes I did.

CONAN DOYLE. He sounded so happy.

LADY JEAN. I know. Wonderful.

HOUDINI *removes* MINA*'s feet from his lap and stands up. His expression is impenetrable.*

MINA. Water. Glass of water, please.

LADY JEAN *kisses the top of* CONAN DOYLE*'s head.*

LADY JEAN (*gently whispered*). I'm so pleased, darling.

HOUDINI *and* BESS *watch* CONAN DOYLE, *this great bear of a man, sobbing his eyes out.*

MINA (*gently*). Sir Arthur?

CONAN DOYLE *looks up at* MINA.

CONAN DOYLE. Thank you.

MINA. Not at all.

CONAN DOYLE (*taking* LADY JEAN*'s hand*). We cannot thank you enough.

MINA. Sir Arthur… (*Searching her conscious memory.*) Was your son… He was here, wasn't he?

CONAN DOYLE. He was.

MINA. I'm so glad. It makes it all worthwhile.

CONAN DOYLE *staggers to his feet,* LADY JEAN *grabs his arm.*

LADY JEAN. I've got you!

CONAN DOYLE *stumbles over to* HOUDINI. *Smiling tearfully he envelops him in a bear hug.*

CONAN DOYLE. My dear sparring partner! We've shared a very sacred moment together.

CONAN DOYLE *stares at his new friend, waiting expectantly.*

Well?

HOUDINI. This was a truly… impressive manifestation.

CONAN DOYLE. Impressive?

HOUDINI. Very impressive.

CONAN DOYLE. Wasn't it evidence enough for you?

Silence. The room waits. Eventually:

HOUDINI. I want to believe. I seek the truth.

CONAN DOYLE. We all seek the truth. You don't doubt what you've just witnessed?

HOUDINI *considers his response.*

HOUDINI. I saw it with my own eyes.

For a second, CONAN DOYLE *is disappointed by this careful ambivalence, but then his habitual credulity and goodwill kick in.*

CONAN DOYLE. We all did! (*Hugging* HOUDINI *again.*) Welcome!

BESS. Give me a hug too, Arthur.

CONAN DOYLE *smiles and envelops the tiny* BESS *in a bear hug.*

I was scared! Weren't you scared?

CONAN DOYLE. Fear was the last thing in my mind! Too happy to be scared!

He holds out his hand to LADY JEAN.

Jean… I think we should give thanks.

CONAN DOYLE *drops his head and closes his eyes.* LADY JEAN, BESS *and the* CRANDONS *follow suit.* HOUDINI *does not. His eyes remain defiantly open.*

Thank you, God, for the blessings you have bestowed upon us, spiritual and temporal. Thank you for the love we have for one another, for our family and friends, both the living and the dead.

The lights fade.

Scene Six

Hours later. The curtains are drawn. Table lamps light the room.

The door opens and HOUDINI *creeps in wearing dressing gown and slippers. Quietly, he closes the door… then moves quickly.*

He kicks off his slippers and jumps onto the séance table. He reaches up and feels inside the overhead lamp. Bingo. A small shower of white rose petals flutter down.

He climbs down and sits at the table, holding out his arms as if gripping his neighbours' hands. He lifts one leg onto the table. He stretches his foot towards the centre of the table and presses down with a single prehensile toe…

… as the door opens. HOUDINI *whips his leg off the table.* CONAN DOYLE *enters, also in dressing gown and slippers.*

CONAN DOYLE. I thought you'd gone to bed.

HOUDINI. Not quite.

CONAN DOYLE. I always think the table has a certain aura after a successful séance.

HOUDINI. I like the table.

CONAN DOYLE. Just the two of us left standing, eh? I'm glad, it's been a wonderful day.

HOUDINI. A very special day.

CONAN DOYLE. May I ask why you came downstairs?

HOUDINI. To relive the afternoon.

CONAN DOYLE. I was wondering if we should draw up a document describing today's séance. We could sign it as witnesses to the veracity of what occurred.

HOUDINI. You want me to sign something?

CONAN DOYLE. Only if you feel able to.

HOUDINI. I am… walking on air, Sir Arthur, but I need a little more time.

CONAN DOYLE. Of course. But now we're alone, you can be truthful. You've nothing to prove to me.

HOUDINI *considers for a moment.*

HOUDINI. I 'observe trifles', to quote your great detective. If I was Sherlock today… I'd want to know why there were rose petals in the lampshade. I'd want to know if it was possible to ring the bell with anything other than your hands. I'd want to know if I could levitate the table with my knee.

CONAN DOYLE. The most underrated trait of Holmes is his incredibly open mind. Remember his credo: 'Exclude the impossible and what is left, *however improbable*, must be the truth.'

HOUDINI. Exactly my point.

They stare at each other in silence.

It's true, it's been a wonderful day. Thank you for inviting us.

CONAN DOYLE. Our pleasure.

HOUDINI. At this exact moment, I'm pinching myself! Here we are sitting together in our bathrobes. The Great Houdini and Sir Arthur Conan Doyle. Are we the two most famous men on the planet?

CONAN DOYLE. You may well be, I wouldn't include myself. We're probably the most celebrated teetotallers on the planet!

CONAN DOYLE *gets up and goes to a drinks cupboard.*

Shall we break our rule this once? In the spirit of communion.

HOUDINI. Not for me. You go ahead.

CONAN DOYLE. I'd love to share a glass with you. I feel safe… if you do.

HOUDINI *considers.*

HOUDINI. What are you offering?

CONAN DOYLE. Scotch whisky.

HOUDINI. Just one.

CONAN DOYLE *pours two whiskies.*

CONAN DOYLE. Why don't you drink?

HOUDINI. Doesn't suit my job. It would be easy to drink to kill the fear, but it's the fear that keeps me alive. What about you?

CONAN DOYLE. My father was an alcoholic. He died in an asylum. The gentlest of men, but a failure.

HOUDINI. My father failed too. A rabbi without a congregation. What did yours do for a living?

CONAN DOYLE. He was a painter of fantastical creatures. Unicorns and fairy kingdoms. Not too far removed from genius.

HOUDINI. So that's where you get it from.

CONAN DOYLE. One of the last things he said to me was: 'There is nothing so sweet in life as leaving it.' I agree with him.

HOUDINI. You're in a hurry to leave this world?

CONAN DOYLE. No, no, no. One world at a time. I love this life, but I look forward to the next.

He hands HOUDINI *his drink and sits on the sofa. He pats the cushion beside him.*

Come and sit beside me.

HOUDINI *sits next to* CONAN DOYLE. *They clink glasses.*

To you, to Bess, to Jean, to Kingsley, to our fathers… to Jack Dempsey the Manassa Mauler.

HOUDINI. L'chaim.

They take a slug and cough and splutter, like two schoolboys tasting alcohol for the first time. They lean against each other, giggling.

How long's it been?

CONAN DOYLE. Years. You?

HOUDINI. Too long to remember.

CONAN DOYLE. Good Lord!

HOUDINI. Gee!

They laugh and take another slug. The effect of the alcohol on these non-drinkers is almost immediate.

CONAN DOYLE. Goodness me!

HOUDINI. Gosh!

CONAN DOYLE. Down in one!

HOUDINI. Down in one!

They knock back their whiskies. CONAN DOYLE *refills their glasses.*

CONAN DOYLE. Here's a question for you, Houdini … happiest moment of your life?

HOUDINI. The day my mother saw me jump. November tenth, 1907, I jumped from Brooklyn Bridge, ninety feet into the East River, chained and cuffed. They smashed a hole in the ice for me to dive into. My mother stood beside me on the bridge and watched me jump. My life was complete.

CONAN DOYLE (*handing* HOUDINI *his refill*). Wonderful.

HOUDINI. What about you?

CONAN DOYLE. This afternoon, without question. I spoke to my son! No further proof needed. The joy! The relief!… Whisky!

He downs his second glass and pours himself a third. He starts to laugh.

Higher! I must climb! I need to climb!

He clambers onto one of the séance table chairs.

I had a classics teacher at school – Pinky Parks we called him – he *loved* teaching and the more excited he got during the lesson, the higher he would climb! He'd climb onto his chair and then onto his desk.

CONAN DOYLE *follows suit and climbs onto the séance table, towering over* HOUDINI.

(*Ecstatic.*) And I know what he means! You have to climb!

CONAN DOYLE *stretches his arms heavenwards.*

Joy!! Joy!! Joooooyyy!!

He looks down at HOUDINI. *He points his finger at him.*

Are you my Doubting Thomas?

HOUDINI. Who are you? Jesus Christ?

CONAN DOYLE. Most loved of the disciples. Come and dance.

CONAN DOYLE *reaches down and takes* HOUDINI*'s hand. He hauls him up onto the séance table.*

HOUDINI. A little drunk.

CONAN DOYLE. Aye, a wee bit blootered!

CONAN DOYLE *hums 'The Blue Danube'* (*or similar*) *and they waltz/stagger round the table.*

Now I have to read you something.

They stop dancing. CONAN DOYLE *takes a newspaper cutting out of his pocket.*

From the *New York Times*, a week ago. I won't attempt the accent: 'In the many séances I have attended, I have never seen or heard anything that could convince me. I know these people – they are cheap magicians, despicable liars, they try tricks I would be ashamed to use on stage.' Who wrote that?

HOUDINI. I did.

CONAN DOYLE. But I don't believe you believe this. You write it to protect yourself. And after this afternoon, you *cannot* fight the truth! So...

CONAN DOYLE *scrunches the newspaper article into a ball.*

...I scrunch this up and bowl it into the void.

He bowls it like a cricket ball into the darkness of the room. The two men stare at each other.

HOUDINI. If believing our loved ones are protected after they have passed on, if that is spiritualism, then I think I believe in it, but if it's founded on feats of magic and trickery, then I say unflinchingly, I do not believe.

CONAN DOYLE (*deal done*). Fair enough. The walls are moving. Must not close my eyes. Whisky! (*Chuckling.*) Whisky.

CONAN DOYLE *plonks himself down and sits on the table.* HOUDINI *sits beside him and rests his head on* CONAN DOYLE*'s shoulder. They sit in silence for a while.*

Speaking to Kingsley isn't only profound for me, it's profound for our children. The war has left a spiritual void which must be filled – but *not* with Christianity. Christianity is DEAD! I hate it. Predicated on guilt, punishment, power.

HOUDINI. And if you're proud to be Jewish?

CONAN DOYLE. Jewish or Christian, our children deserve a new religion, which bridges the gap between the physics of Einstein and the poetry of faith. Spiritualism does that.

Silence.

HOUDINI. I admire you more than Picasso… or Stravinsky… or the Human Fly.

Silence.

CONAN DOYLE. Did you love your mother unreservedly?

HOUDINI. Unreservedly. You?

CONAN DOYLE. Unreservedly.

HOUDINI. I wrote a poem. Can I recite it to you?

CONAN DOYLE. Please.

HOUDINI.
'I have wandered wide and far
On ocean wave and whirling car
But in my memory your image is engraven deep
Mama – come back and rock me to sleep.'

CONAN DOYLE. I like it.

HOUDINI *crumples. His turn to cry. He buries his head in* CONAN DOYLE*'s chest.* CONAN DOYLE *puts an arm round him.* HOUDINI *looks like a small boy.*

We'll find your mother. Don't you worry. We'll find her.

HOUDINI *cries,* CONAN DOYLE *comforts him.*

Blackout.

End of Act One.

Interval.

ACT TWO

Scene One

Months later.

... A scene in which magic occurs.

... in which truth is questionable and events are too fast or too slow.

An 8' by 10' cabinet – centre-stage. Like a miniature theatre: proscenium arch and red-velvet curtain.

BESS *enters carrying a rolled-up sack.*

HOUDINI *enters.*

BESS *places the sack in front of* HOUDINI. *He steps into it. She pulls the sack up over* HOUDINI*'s head and ties it at the top.*

Two ASSISTANTS *enter, carrying a large trunk. They place it on the ground and lift* HOUDINI *into it. They close the lid and lock it.*

The ASSISTANTS *place the trunk in the cabinet.* BESS *steps into the cabinet and stands beside the trunk. She closes the curtain. From behind the curtain she claps three times:*

One – two – three.

The curtain whips open and HOUDINI, *not* BESS, *steps out.*

The ASSISTANTS *lift the trunk out of the cabinet. They unlock it and lift out the sack, still firmly tied at the top. They untie it and let it fall... revealing... not* BESS*... but in an explosion of light and colour,* CONAN DOYLE. *He's dressed in white tie and tails. Pleased with himself, he flings his arms wide, Houdini-style.*

HOUDINI *snaps his fingers and a luminous trumpet appears. The three valves rise and fall of their own volition.* CONAN DOYLE *snaps his fingers – a tambourine whizzes through the air, rattling its cymbals.*

Blackout.

Scene Two

The Doyles and Houdinis have rented an apartment by the sea on Long Island. A sun-drenched living room with a patio overlooking the Atlantic Ocean.

An open suitcase on the floor, a half-finished game of cards on a table. Doors off, on opposite sides of the room.

BESS *lies on a sofa,* LADY JEAN *sits in an armchair.*

BESS (*sleepily*). Okay, this is the first line:
(*Singing.*) 'Rosabelle, sweet Rosabelle…'

LADY JEAN (*singing beautifully*).
'Rosabelle, sweet Rosabelle…'

BESS *sits up abruptly. Amazed.*

BESS. Hey Jean! You are good! (*Singing the next line.*)
'I love you more than I can tell…'

LADY JEAN (*sung*).
'I love you more than I can tell…'

BESS (*sung*).
'O'er me you cast a spell,
I love you my sweet Rosabelle.'

LADY JEAN (*sung*).
'O'er me you cast a spell…'

BESS/LADY JEAN (*together*).
'I love you my sweet Rosabelle.'

BESS. What a beautiful voice!

LADY JEAN. Well… in another life, you know…

BESS. Cat's pyjamas!

LADY JEAN. I rather envy *your* life.

BESS. Don't! It's all crazy bull.

LADY JEAN. Performing though…

BESS. Not as fun as it looks.

LADY JEAN. I actually read music at the Guildhall School of Music.

BESS. What do ya know!

LADY JEAN. I always wanted to sing… and act a little. I've been to three musical plays in the West End this year, musicals they're called now, and several of my contemporaries were performing, it was nice to catch up.

BESS. Do you regret it?

LADY JEAN. Regret what?

BESS. Not singing professionally.

LADY JEAN (*instantly vehement*). No! NO! NO!! Of course not!

BESS. Okay.

LADY JEAN. I would never have met Arthur. And there are more important things! We have so much work to do, Bess, *vital* work, you know that, of course I don't regret it.

BESS. Sure.

LADY JEAN. Not at all! It's just nice sometimes… to…

BESS. I get ya. (*A beat.*) Shall we put in some harmonies?

LADY JEAN (*a little unsettled*). I would love to, at some point, but do you know, I'm *so* hot, I think I'll change into something cooler.

BESS. Okay. You say when, an' we'll have a sing-song.

LADY JEAN. Absolutely.

LADY JEAN *goes in to the Doyles' bedroom.* BESS *lies down again. She closes her eyes and hums 'Rosabelle'.*

CONAN DOYLE *and* HOUDINI *enter carrying golf clubs.* BESS *opens her eyes, otherwise she doesn't move.*

BESS. Who won?

HOUDINI. Honey, Arthur is what he calls a scratch golfer. I can hardly hit the ball, it's not a question of winning or losing.

BESS. But you had a good time?

CONAN DOYLE. We did indeed.

BESS. Did you argue?

Silence says 'yes'.

(*Exasperated.*) Oh why? So stupid! Stop it! Both of you!

CONAN DOYLE. Not an argument, a discussion.

HOUDINI. Animated.

CONAN DOYLE. Exactly.

HOUDINI *sits on the vacant sunbed.* CONAN DOYLE *stands – something is irritating him.*

BESS. You wanna sit down?

CONAN DOYLE. I'm fine, thank you.

Silence in the heat.

BESS (*to 'defrost' the atmosphere*). Do the 'clubs', Arthur.

HOUDINI (*suddenly chuckling*). Yeah! Do the golf clubs!

BESS. Please!

CONAN DOYLE *thaws.*

CONAN DOYLE (*faux irritation*). Pass me my clubs then.

BESS. Yeahhh!

BESS *jumps to her feet and hands* CONAN DOYLE *his golf bag.*

CONAN DOYLE. It requires a moment of preparation.

He clamps his golf bag between his legs. He then proceeds to name each club, lifting it out of the bag and slotting it back at huge speed:

Driver, brassie, spoon, baffie, cleek, mashie, niblick, jigger and putter. (*Even quicker.*) Driver, brassie, spoon, baffie, cleek, mashie, niblick, jigger and putter.

CONAN DOYLE *holds the last club, the putter aloft.* BESS *claps her hands,* HOUDINI *laughs.*

BESS. I love that!

HOUDINI. Is that a Scottish accent?

CONAN DOYLE. It is. You can't do the clubs in an English accent. It's an insult to the origins of the game.

BESS. And you're Scottish?

CONAN DOYLE. Well my parents were originally from Ireland, but I was brought up in Scotland.

HOUDINI. But you don't have an accent.

CONAN DOYLE. No, I was sent to a Catholic boarding school in Lancashire, a *barbaric* institution, they knocked the accent out of me.

BESS. Well I love the clubs, do them one last time.

CONAN DOYLE. Driver, brassie, spoon, baffie, cleek, mashie, niblick, jigger and putter!

HOUDINI. Niblick.

CONAN DOYLE. Niblick.

BESS. Niblick, niblick.

HOUDINI/BESS/ARTHUR. Niblick, niblick, nibble, bibble, ibble, biblick, niblick.

HOUDINI. You know what we call golf clubs in the States, Bess?

BESS. No, but you're gonna tell me.

HOUDINI. One, two, three, four, five, six, seven, eight and nine. Can you believe that? A bunch of numbers. What is it with Americans?

BESS. Your kids play, Arthur?

CONAN DOYLE. Kingsley did. On the day he went to the Front, he made a pact with me: 'If I'm killed, Father, we'll meet on the fourth green on the first anniversary of my death.' The fourth was our favourite hole at the Crowborough Beacon Golf Course. So a year to the day after his death, Jean packed me some sandwiches and I spent a day and a night on the fourth green. The greenkeeper found me the next morning asleep in the bunker.

HOUDINI. Your son didn't show up?

CONAN DOYLE. Not on that occasion.

HOUDINI. Maybe he couldn't find his niblick on the other side.

An ugly silence.

CONAN DOYLE. That is a cheap jibe.

BESS. Oh Harry…

CONAN DOYLE. That was beneath you.

BESS. Apologise, honey.

CONAN DOYLE. Ever since I last saw you, you've continued to write articles and make speeches criticising me, criticising the integrity of mediums all over the world.

HOUDINI. The integrity of mediums, yes, I never criticise you.

CONAN DOYLE. You criticise people I respect.

HOUDINI. It's the fakes I can't stand.

CONAN DOYLE. You and I witnessed a séance of incontrovertible power. And I watched you, you were as white as a sheet, extremely moved, and you used a phrase, I will never forget it, you said you were 'walking on air'. Do you remember saying that?

HOUDINI. It was a long time ago, Sir Arthur.

CONAN DOYLE. You said you were 'walking on air'.

HOUDINI. Maybe.

CONAN DOYLE. Was Mina Crandon's work that day not proof enough for you?

HOUDINI. No it was not.

CONAN DOYLE. What failed to convince you?

HOUDINI. Nothing convinced me.

CONAN DOYLE. But your denial's a form of insanity.

HOUDINI. Let's not talk about this now.

CONAN DOYLE. How could you possibly doubt it?

HOUDINI. Please, Arthur…

BESS. Boys, it's too hot to fight.

HOUDINI. I wanna talk about Sir Arthur Conan Doyle's triumphant return to New York City. Carnegie Hall sold out!

CONAN DOYLE. It may have been sold out, but my audience was thoroughly disappointed. They thought I was here to talk about Sherlock Holmes, they weren't expecting a lecture on the spirit world.

Short silence.

BESS. Arthur?

CONAN DOYLE. Bess.

BESS. I believed Mina Crandon.

CONAN DOYLE. I find it inconceivable that anybody who witnesses her powers would not believe.

BESS. There's something I don't get though. It confuses me.

CONAN DOYLE. Fire away.

BESS. Your first wife Louisa passed away…

CONAN DOYLE. Yes.

BESS. And I'm so sorry about that.

CONAN DOYLE. Don't be.

BESS. And now thank God you've met Jean…

CONAN DOYLE. Yes.

BESS. Okay. This is what troubles me: who gets the guy in the spirit world?

CONAN DOYLE (*guarded*). I don't understand you.

BESS. Well, when you and Jean arrive in the spirit world, ain't Louisa gonna want a bit of the action?

Unnoticed, LADY JEAN *has rejoined them on the patio.*

LADY JEAN. Not once in the fourteen years since she died, has Louisa tried to contact Arthur. Not once. At best I would call that careless. Spiritualists are very clear on the issue: true love is eternal in the spirit world, the institution of marriage comes a poor second.

BESS. So you win?

LADY JEAN. You have a rather blunt way of expressing yourself.

BESS. I know. (*A beat, then.*) Two girls, three boys! Gee! I would like to have had kids.

LADY JEAN. It's not too late.

BESS. Honey, I ain't had a red wedding for ten years.

LADY JEAN *looks confused.*

A period. And no bubs, as you can see.

She places a hand on her flat chest.

The whole shebang's probably my fault.

LADY JEAN *looks shocked.*

Too blunt again huh? (*Short silence.*) No, no kids. We have a make-believe son though, don't we, Harry? He's a clever boy, went to Harvard, did all different jobs, he was an actor, a baseball player, a teacher, now he's the President of the United States! I'm working on him – (*Holding up her bottle of beer.*) I want him to end prohibition! Harry Junior we call him. (*Short silence.*) Harry's mom prayed every day for us to have kids. I prayed too. Too bad.

CONAN DOYLE. It *is* too bad.

HOUDINI. Which is worse? Not to have a child, or to lose one so young.

CONAN DOYLE. You're asking the wrong person. I know Kingsley is happy, I miss him, of course, but I no longer grieve.

HOUDINI. I gotta a little girl in my life anyway, called Bess.

BESS. Don't kid yourself, Harry, I'm the parent round here.

Short silence.

LADY JEAN (*holding up a pad of paper and pencil*). Actually I came back to suggest I might try a little writing. For you, Houdini. I sense a force urging me to try. To contact your mother perhaps?

CONAN DOYLE *turns to* HOUDINI.

CONAN DOYLE. Would you like to?

HOUDINI *says nothing.*

A chance to begin the search.

HOUDINI*'s heart beats hard.*

HOUDINI. It's my mother's birthday today. Did you know that?

CONAN DOYLE. I had no idea.

HOUDINI. Kind of a strange coincidence.

CONAN DOYLE. I had no idea at all.

CONAN DOYLE *takes* LADY JEAN*'s hand.*

Did you know?

LADY JEAN. No I didn't.

CONAN DOYLE. Isn't this an opportunity, Houdini? On such an auspicious day.

LADY JEAN. I can't promise, but I'm usually right, aren't I, Arthur?

CONAN DOYLE. You're always right.

LADY JEAN (*a sweet smile*). I think I told you, my hand starts to tingle.

BESS. You should try, honey.

CONAN DOYLE (*to* HOUDINI.) I understand your anxiety.

HOUDINI. I'm not anxious.

CONAN DOYLE. Good. (*A beat, then.*) I trust Jean with my life, you couldn't be in safer hands.

Silence.

HOUDINI (*almost whispered*). I seek the truth.

CONAN DOYLE (*placing a hand on* HOUDINI*'s shoulder*). Shall we?

CONAN DOYLE *and* LADY JEAN *wait for* HOUDINI*'s decision. Finally:*

HOUDINI. Sure.

CONAN DOYLE *sits at the table.*

CONAN DOYLE. Let's sit.

LADY JEAN *and* HOUDINI *join him. As one, they suddenly remember* BESS. *They turn to her.*

BESS. You know, fellas, I'm gonna butt out. Don't want nothin' to spoil the… the scripting. I'm gonna cop a snooze. Can't wait to hear all about it, Harry.

HOUDINI. See you soon, honey.

BESS *goes in to the Houdinis' bedroom.*

Do I have to do anything?

LADY JEAN. Nothing at all. Do you have any questions?

HOUDINI *shakes his head. With great reverence,* LADY JEAN *picks up a pencil in her right hand. She pulls a pad of paper towards her. Then with a self-deprecating smile, she nods to* CONAN DOYLE.

CONAN DOYLE. Oh God, protect us as we seek, in good faith, contact with loved ones on the other side of the veil.

Silence. They wait. HOUDINI*'s concentration is intense; he desperately wants to believe.*

Suddenly LADY JEAN*'s right hand jerks spasmodically.*

LADY JEAN. Oh. Oh, oh.

She closes her eyes. Her hand leaps into the air.

I have… never… never… felt such force.

CONAN DOYLE *places a comforting hand on her shoulder.*

CONAN DOYLE. Easy now.

LADY JEAN (*to the 'spirit force'*). Wait! Wait! Whoever you are… do you believe in God?

The spirit answers by slamming LADY JEAN*'s hand down on the table three times. She gasps.*

Thank you. Then I will make the sign of the cross.

She draws a cross on the first sheet of paper then tears it off the pad. Her hand hovers.

(*To the spirit.*) Are you Houdini's mother?

HOUDINI (*almost inaudible*). Mama, are you here?

Again the spirit slams LADY JEAN*'s hand down on the table three times.*

CONAN DOYLE. Three times is 'yes'.

Suddenly the pencil dives and LADY JEAN *writes frantically. The graduate of the Guildhall School of Music and Drama speaks as she writes.*

LADY JEAN (*using her own voice, but with great fervour*). Oh my darling, at last I'm through – I've tried so often – my beloved boy, don't grieve – I am so happy in this life – all sweetness around one – I love you more than ever…

LADY JEAN *tears off a sheet of paper.* CONAN DOYLE *strokes her hair.*

CONAN DOYLE. Do you want to ask your mother a question?

HOUDINI *shakes his head. His expression is grim.*

You could ask whether she can read your mind.

LADY JEAN (*writing again*). Of course I can read his mind – Soon, my son, you will get all the evidence you need.

LADY JEAN *pauses again. Her hand hovers.*

(*Writing again.*) God bless you too, Sir Arthur, for helping us to contact our beloved ones on the earth plane.

CONAN DOYLE *smiles modestly. Another sheet is torn off.*

– You remembered my birthday, Harry!

CONAN DOYLE *places his hand gently on* HOUDINI*'s shoulder, his other hand still rests on his wife's shoulder. An image of 'Christ-like' protection.*

Thank you for remembering. I want you to know my son, I have bridged the gulf and I am happy, that is what I wanted to tell you – now I can rest in peace.

LADY JEAN *drops the pencil. She's exhausted.*

CONAN DOYLE. Thank you, Jean.

He touches her flushed cheek affectionately. HOUDINI *cannot speak.*

Houdini?

Still no response. Long silence, then slowly HOUDINI *gets to his feet.* LADY JEAN *watches him expectantly.*

HOUDINI. Please! Excuse me… I… I… need…

He stumbles away from the table – and out onto the patio. LADY JEAN *looks anxiously at* CONAN DOYLE. CONAN DOYLE *smiles reassuringly. He lifts* LADY JEAN*'s hand and very gently kisses it.*

LADY JEAN (*seeking approbation*). Did I…

CONAN DOYLE. You are a wonderful, wonderful woman.

CONAN DOYLE *leads* LADY JEAN *to the edge of the stage. They watch* HOUDINI.

HOUDINI *sinks to his knees and looks out to sea. We hear the crash of Atlantic breakers.*

HOUDINI. Mama's last kiss. Her dry lips on my cheek. I feel them now. Her lips stick to my skin as they pull away.

A white-hot anger builds in HOUDINI.

I am strong enough, others are not. I cannot… allow… any longer… the time has come.

With furious intensity, HOUDINI *hurls furniture offstage. He destroys the set.* BESS *returns, alarmed by the noise. She, like* CONAN DOYLE *and* LADY JEAN, *watches from the edge of the stage.*

HOUDINI *turns to face the audience. A placard appears above his head. It reads: 'HILL STREET THEATRE, LOS ANGELES, JUNE 1923.'*

Ladies and gentlemen, I have embarked on this series of lectures for the sake of the vulnerable, for those who are brought to the brink of insanity by their desire to communicate with the dead. I have studied mediums, I'm the Magic Man, I'm the King of Illusion, I see through these fakes!

CONAN DOYLE *watches* HOUDINI *speak, increasingly angry.*

I speak for those who seek the truth and nothing but the truth.

CONAN DOYLE *has had enough. He rejoins the action, also addressing the audience. A placard above his head reads: 'CARNEGIE HALL, NEW YORK CITY. JUNE 1923.'*

CONAN DOYLE. Ladies and gentlemen, I speak to those who long with all their sad hearts to communicate with loved ones who have passed over. The work I am doing is the greatest humanitarian achievement of my life.

HOUDINI. The work I am doing is the greatest humanitarian achievement of my life…

CONAN DOYLE *and* HOUDINI (*in unison*). Aggressive fighting for right is the noblest sport the world affords.

CONAN DOYLE *and* HOUDINI *look across at each other.* (*'Yes we both believe that.'*)

Any questions?

AUDIENCE MEMBER 1 (*to* HOUDINI). Are you at war with Sir Arthur Conan Doyle?

HOUDINI. No, he is a dear friend. He is sincere in everything he says and does.

CONAN DOYLE (*pointing at an audience member with their hand raised*). Yes?

AUDIENCE MEMBER 2. Is your friendship with Harry Houdini over?

CONAN DOYLE. No, he is a dear friend. He is sincere in everything he says and does.

The placards discard another sheet. The next sheets both read: 'DENVER, SEPTEMBER 1923.'

I respect his beliefs.

HOUDINI. I listen to his views with an open mind, but Sir Arthur Conan Doyle plays a dangerous game. A week ago, here in Denver, a mother and her seven-year-old son attended a lecture by Sir Arthur. The mother was so moved, so desperate to reach the spirit world, that she rushed home with her son, shot the boy through the head then turned the gun on herself.

This is too much for CONAN DOYLE. *He is so angry that he turns away from the audience and faces* HOUDINI.

CONAN DOYLE. Are you saying I was complicit in this woman's death?

HOUDINI. I'm saying you… and your wife… play a dangerous game.

CONAN DOYLE. You're suggesting my wife is in some way responsible? That is a disgusting implication. Take it back.

HOUDINI. I cannot.

CONAN DOYLE. You're implying that Jean is dishonest.

CONAN DOYLE *and* HOUDINI *are no longer making speeches, they are arguing in the same room.*

LADY JEAN *steps 'in stage' and joins* CONAN DOYLE.

HOUDINI. I hold you both in the highest esteem…

LADY JEAN. Clearly not.

CONAN DOYLE. I have witnessed many times the purity of Jean's mediumship.

HOUDINI. I'm not questioning Lady Jean's sincerity.

CONAN DOYLE. That is precisely what you're questioning. You are inferring that my wife, my *wife*, Houdini, is a fraud. And that I will not stand for.

HOUDINI. I wanted to hear Ma's voice, on her birthday, what a wonderful thing that would have been. I passionately wanted to believe.

LADY JEAN. She was in the room with us.

HOUDINI. No she was not. You wrote a cross on the top of the first page. My mother was Jewish.

CONAN DOYLE. And if Jean had been a Jewish medium, it would have been the Star of David and not a cross.

LADY JEAN. I always write a cross on the first page. To ward off demons, who would if they could, destroy the message.

HOUDINI. The message which was written entirely in English. My mother was Hungarian, she spoke Yiddish, for God's sake! Couldn't read, write, or speak the English language. Not a word. Not a *single word.*

CONAN DOYLE (*softly, persuasively*). Do you really think that in the afterlife, individual languages are a barrier to communication? Of course the message was in English. We three are English speakers.

HOUDINI (*very, very angry, but controlled*). In your message my mother called me Harry. My name is Eric Weiss. Not Harry Houdini. Mama called me Eric. *Always.*

CONAN DOYLE. But Jean knows you as Harry. Why would your mother want to confuse her medium?

HOUDINI. The words in your message were sentimental generalities. Crass and banal. It was not my mother speaking.

LADY JEAN. You are implying I am dishonest.

HOUDINI. No.

CONAN DOYLE (*furious*). You certainly are.

There is a steely coldness in LADY JEAN*'s expression.*

LADY JEAN. Why would I lie to you?

HOUDINI. I believe you are sincere. But you love your husband.

LADY JEAN (*self-evident*). Yes.

HOUDINI. You do it for his benefit.

LADY JEAN (*pale with anger*). If I was strong enough, I would knock you down.

CONAN DOYLE. That's a disgraceful suggestion.

HOUDINI. I believe it's true.

CONAN DOYLE. Apologise to my wife.

HOUDINI. No.

LADY JEAN. This isn't a game, you know, what you are implying is blasphemous. We are a powerful movement. There are a good number of people who are extremely annoyed by what you say in public. You should be careful.

On that forbidding note, LADY JEAN *turns and walks offstage*. BESS *gets up*.

BESS. Very goddamn unnecessary, Harry.

She hurries after LADY JEAN.

CONAN DOYLE. You have insulted my wife and therefore me.

HOUDINI. Not my intention.

CONAN DOYLE. How long our friendship can survive this ordeal, I do not know.

HOUDINI. Do you really believe that tables lifting up and down in the dark, or tambourines flying through the air, are messages from God?

CONAN DOYLE. We draw our knowledge from our loved ones who have passed over and if sometimes they choose simple physical manifestations to prove life after death, then I'm grateful to them. And of course there are frauds and charlatans, fakery has existed in every religion since the beginning of time, but there are also many profound and sincere mediums. I hate it when you simplify and generalise.

HOUDINI. I wouldn't mind if it cost a couple of bucks on a seaside pier… but it doesn't, millions and millions of dollars are thrown away in séances every week.

CONAN DOYLE. You reduce everything to the financial…

HOUDINI. Okay, here's the financial, here's the fucking financial! I will pay you…

CONAN DOYLE. I don't want your money.

HOUDINI. Not you, I will pay your Society for Psychical Research…

CONAN DOYLE. Here you go again.

HOUDINI.…if Mina Crandon can prove conclusively that she has supernatural powers.

CONAN DOYLE. She certainly won't want your payment.

HOUDINI (*drumming it in*). Not *you*, not *her*, the money goes to the SPR. Think of the publicity.

Silence.

CONAN DOYLE (*almost whispered*). Six times I have spoken face to face with my son,

HOUDINI. No you haven't.

CONAN DOYLE (*almost too angry to continue*). Twice with my mother, once with my brother, all in their own voices and on private matters, so for me there is not, nor has been for a long time, any doubt. I *know* it is true.

HOUDINI. No.

CONAN DOYLE. What do you mean 'no'?

HOUDINI. You're all fakes. You're a menace to mankind.

Too much for CONAN DOYLE. *He launches a punch at* HOUDINI, *but* HOUDINI *parries the blow and ducks under* CONAN DOYLE*'s guard. He hits* CONAN DOYLE *hard in the stomach.* CONAN DOYLE *gasps, he grabs* HOUDINI *by the shoulder, holds him at arm's length, clenches his fist and prepares to knock him senseless.* HOUDINI *raises his fists in preparation to defend.*

But instead of punches, they lurch forward and grab each other. They wrestle. They crash to the ground and roll across the floor.

Eventually, exhausted, they stop fighting and lie facing each other – forehead to forehead. They rub their heads together, as if forcing their passion into the other man's skull. Then they flop onto their backs, still gasping for breath.

CONAN DOYLE. Why? Why do we…? What can we do? We should be friends.

HOUDINI. We are friends. I dunno what we do.

They recover their breath. CONAN DOYLE *feels for* HOUDINI*'s hand.*

A long silence.

CONAN DOYLE. We loved our mothers. And we lost them. We both know… that to lose someone is to understand, emotionally not intellectually, that you will never, *never* see that person again. You are trampling on those people's hopes, Houdini. Exacerbating their suffering. And I'm warning you as your friend, many people are very, very angry.

Blackout.

Scene Three

A theatre. The sound of a mutinous audience. HOUDINI *loyalists are shouting: 'HOUDINI! HOUDINI! HOUDINI!' But there are angry hecklers out there too: 'BLASPHEMER! BLASPHEMER! BLASPHEMER!'*

HOUDINI *is about to do his act. He's in the wings, preparing to go on stage.* BESS *is beside him.*

HOUDINI. They're coming for me, Bess. I'm telling ya, only a matter of time.

BESS. You don't have to go on stage, Harry, you don't have to. We can cancel.

They listen anxiously as the hecklers get louder: 'GOD WILL PUNISH YOU!! GOD WILL DESTROY YOU!!'

BESS *is holding a sheet of writing paper.*

This letter is not nice. We gotta take it to the cops. If you think there's someone out there, don't go on.

HOUDINI. There's always someone out there. Maybe today, maybe tomorrow, nothing we can do.

HOUDINI *suddenly sinks to his knees and prays to his mother.* BESS *crouches beside him.*

Ma? You'll tell me, won't you? You'll warn me if I'm in trouble? Look after me, Ma, don't let me make a fool of myself. Ma? Can you hear me?

BESS. I'm gonna tell them you're not going on.

HOUDINI. Ma – can you answer me?

BESS *starts to go, but* HOUDINI *grabs her wrist.*

Wait, Bess!

BESS. Baby, let's cancel.

HOUDINI (*looking up*). I heard the voice! I heard you, Ma! Thank you, thank you!

BESS. Come away, sweetheart!

HOUDINI. NO! It's okay! I'll be okay. They're only after me because they're runnin' scared.

He pulls himself to his feet, empties his pockets of magician's paraphernalia and thrusts it into BESS*'s hands.*

BESS. What you doin'?

HOUDINI. They don't deserve me. No magic, Bess. I won't perform to liars! But if they want the truth, they will get the truth, I will tell them the truth.

BESS *grabs his arm, but* HOUDINI *shakes himself free.*

The Great Houdini will not let the dragon prevail!

He strides onto the stage. The hecklers are screaming for blood.

(*To the audience, messianic.*) LIARS! You are LIARS! *Truth is the only real magic!* The dragon I am engaged with, dwells in an undrained swamp! I have invaded the morass and annoyed the monster!

HECKLERS. Blasphemer! Blasphemer!

HOUDINI. What type of a ghoul seeks profit from the dead?

HECKLERS. God will punish you!

HOUDINI. I will shout the truth from the rooftops! There are only three kinds of medium: psychotics, criminals and the deluded!

HECKLERS. We will protect our God!

HOUDINI. I will protect the public!

HECKLERS. God will destroy you!

HOUDINI. You are all deluded. You are afraid of dying! I am not afraid!!

He punches the air:

The Great Houdini issues a challenge! I will pay twenty thousand bucks to anyone who can prove to me that mediums have supernatural powers. Are you listening, Arthur Conan Doyle?! Are you listening, Mina Crandon?! But you gotta prove it in front of a panel of top-notch scientists and rep-resentatives of the *New York Times*. I want you to take my dough, I want to make you rich, but you gotta prove it con-clusively! Scien-tifically!

Blackout.

Scene Four

The October 2nd Séance.

A single light focuses on a black-leather briefcase. It snaps open to reveal $20,000 in cash. The greenbacks are vivid in the spotlight.

HOUDINI *picks up the briefcase.*

HOUDINI. Arthur?

CONAN DOYLE *reluctantly joins* HOUDINI. *They stand either side of the money and pose. A pop and flash as an early camera photographs the two men and the booty.*

MINA *is already sitting at a large round table. Hair down, no make-up, black kimono – little else. The red lamp already shines spectrally on her face. The bellbox is in the middle of the table.*

The photo-shoot is over. Everyone approaches the table. A panel of severe-looking scientists sit on the fringes of the room to watch proceedings.

DR CRANDON. Sir Arthur, if you would sit on Mina's left, I will sit on her right…

HOUDINI. No. I arrange the seating.

DR CRANDON. Pardon me?

HOUDINI. I arrange the seating.

LADY JEAN. Why should you?

MINA. Dr Crandon and I were extremely reluctant to take part in a séance predicated on financial gain. However, Sir Arthur has assured us that the benefits for the spiritualist movement are so great that on this one occasion we are prepared to make an exception. *But* if you are coercive and dictatorial, Mr Houdini –

HOUDINI. Not my intention at all.

MINA. If you are in any way tyrannical, it's very unlikely we will make contact with the other side. Success depends on an atmosphere which is spiritually conducive – calm, generous and positive. Is that clear… Houdini?

HOUDINI. I'm on your side, Mrs Crandon, but I still arrange the seating.

Short silence.

DR CRANDON. What did you have in mind?

HOUDINI. I will sit to Mina's left. My wife, Bess, will sit to her right.

MINA. No. Leroy always sits to my right. I require that reassurance.

HOUDINI. I bet you do. Okay, we'll do it this way. Would you like to sit down, Dr Crandon?

DR CRANDON *does not like being told what to do, nevertheless he sits next to his wife.*

Take your wife's hand.

DR CRANDON *does so.*

Bess, I'd like you to stand behind Dr and Mrs Crandon and place your hand on top of theirs. Please don't move from that position at any point during the séance. Arthur, if you sit next to me. Lady Jean, between Dr Crandon and your husband. You gotta realise, I want this to succeed. Normally, I would tie Dr and Mrs Crandon to their chairs.

LADY JEAN. How ridiculous.

MINA. In which case we would abandon the séance.

HOUDINI. But I ain't gonna do it.

CONAN DOYLE (*indignant*). Completely unnecessary.

HOUDINI. I'm just saying that normally in a psychic investigation, I tie the medium to their chair. (*Increasingly wired.*) I would be doing this for your sakes. I don't want these gentlemen – (*Gesturing to the screen.*) to think for a second that you produce phenomena by sleight of hand. I wanna hand over the twenty grand. This is what none of you understand, I *want* to be convinced!

CONAN DOYLE. I know you do.

HOUDINI (*trying so hard to stay calm*). So. Please. *No one* lets go of anybody's hand during the proceedings. *No one* leaves their seat. And with your permission, I would also like to continue with the lights on.

DR CRANDON. No.

HOUDINI. Why not?

DR CRANDON. Darkness is more conducive…

HOUDINI. Why? Why is it more conducive? What difference could it possibly make? Seriously, as an objective observer, I'd like to know.

MINA. My brother Walter only ever comes through under cover of darkness.

HOUDINI. And why is that? Does he have a nervous disposition? He seemed pretty darned confident to me.

DR CRANDON. I think in this atmosphere of suspicion, it is highly unlikely we will achieve anything positive.

CONAN DOYLE. I agree.

HOUDINI. But let's try. Okay? Listen, listen, I'm sorry, You gotta forgive me, I'm giving the wrong impression. Let's try.

HOUDINI *leans across to the middle of the table and hits the bellbox a couple of times.*

Bell's working. Good. Let's sit.

They all look reluctant to proceed.

Seriously, let's sit. Please, I didn't mean to sound negative.

CONAN DOYLE. Houdini. Try to be open, will you? For me. For your sparring partner.

HOUDINI. Sure, I am one thousand per cent open. I still hope 'n' pray, Arthur, you know I do. Let's sit.

They take their places.

As before, Mrs Crandon, if you put your feet in my lap, then I know for sure you're not on the move.

MINA *places her naked feet on* HOUDINI*'s knee.*

(*Resting his hands on her feet.*) Your apple sauce don't touch me – there's no deceiving Houdini.

MINA. I've no desire to deceive you.

Everyone seems ready, BESS *stands behind the* CRANDONS*, her hand covering their joined hands.*

CONAN DOYLE. Before we pray, I would like to quote George Eliot, the wisest woman ever to put pen to paper. (*Looking straight at* HOUDINI.) She wrote: 'Receptiveness is a rare and massive power.' I believe that too. Jean, would you like to lead the prayer?

LADY JEAN. Of course. Oh God, protect us as we seek to travel behind the veil. Help us to believe in your divine presence, through your disciples on the other side, Amen.

The red lamp flicks out. Complete darkness. A long fruitless silence.

MINA. This is very hard. The vibrations are thin.

DR CRANDON (*gently*). Do you wish to stop?

MINA (*after a pause, a small voice*). No. Let's continue.

The silence resumes, but then a tiny sound. The table begins to jolt. Increasingly loudly, the table bangs up and down. And now the bellbox rings… It's a completely different bell, higher-pitched, but it rings several times.

Suddenly there is an almighty kerfuffle under the table – a female scream, the sounds of a struggle. A male voice: 'I got ya!' A female voice: 'Let go!'

HOUDINI. *NOW, BESS!*

The lights come on – brutal, white light. BESS *has moved away from the table and on* HOUDINI*'s instruction, turned on the lights.*

MINA*'s head is under the table,* HOUDINI *has grabbed her hair.* DR CRANDON *is leaning over the table, his hand near the bell, his right hand is still gripping* LADY JEAN*'s.*

Look where I found this bitch!

HOUDINI *drags* MINA *by her hair out from under the table. He pulls her violently across the room and presents her first to the four scientists, who look horrified.*

Look where I found this whore!

HOUDINI *parades* MINA *round the room. He shoves her in front of* CONAN DOYLE.

This bitch was lifting the table with her goddamn head!

MINA. Get your hands off me!

HOUDINI. Stand still!

BESS. Harry, let her go.

MINA. Get your damned hands off me!

MINA *is pounding* HOUDINI *with her fists, scratching at his face.*

HOUDINI. And what are you doing on your feet, Dr Crandon? Show everyone your hands, Leroy.

LADY JEAN *backs away from the table. She looks terrified.* CONAN DOYLE *is utterly shocked.*

MINA. Let go of my hair!

HOUDINI *grips even harder,* MINA *screams.*

HOUDINI. She was pushing the table up and down with her head, nothing slicker than that, with – her – head!

DR CRANDON *is frozen, standing by his chair.*

Show us your hands, Dr Crandon.

But suddenly, out of MINA*'s mouth comes the visceral, guttural sound of her spirit guide, her brother* WALTER*'s voice. Like a malevolent devil buried in her guts.*

WALTER/MINA (*growled aggression*). Get the hell outta here, you son of a bitch! Get the hell outta here, you evil bastard!

HOUDINI. Hello, Walter.

MINA *scratches at* HOUDINI*'s face again.*

WALTER/MINA. You evil fucker, Houdini! Why don't you go back to your Jewish slum in Buda-fucking-pest! Fucking kike!

HOUDINI. That's sweet of you, Walter, so now you don't mind the daylight.

WALTER/MINA. You keep your filthy hands off my sister. Go home, motherfucker! And from what I heard, that's probably what you did.

HOUDINI *hurls* MINA *across the room. She crashes to the floor.*

Before this year is over, you will be dead!

DR CRANDON *is backing away from the table.*

HOUDINI. Hey, hey, hey!

HOUDINI *races round and grabs* DR CRANDON.

Show us your hands, Leroy.

DR CRANDON *has his fists clenched shut.* HOUDINI *forces a hand open and holds it up. The hand is smeared with a black substance.*

Shoe polish. All over his hand. Where'd that come from?

He pushes DR CRANDON *away.*

Have a look at this.

HOUDINI *lifts up the bellbox on the table. He wipes the top of the box with the palm of his hand. Now his hand is covered in black shoe polish.*

So who's been ringing the bell? I switched the boxes.

He presses the bell.

Doesn't have the same tone. Does it?

He reaches under the table and pulls out the original box. He places them side by side on the table. He rings the original bell.

Better.

HOUDINI *walks over to* CONAN DOYLE, *stands over him.* CONAN DOYLE *looks like a defeated schoolboy.*

So that was Walter. Called me a motherfucker and a fucking kike. That's the gentle soul who brought your son back to life.

BESS (*she's had enough*). Harry. (*Grabbing his arm.*) Come away.

HOUDINI. Let go of me, honey, this has to be done.

BESS (*steely*). It does *not* have to be done.

HOUDINI. Hey, Arthur, you still convinced you spoke to Kingsley?

BESS. Stop it. Come away.

HOUDINI. Courtesy of these cheats, these fakes? You still believe you talked to your son?

CONAN DOYLE *has covered his eyes with his hands like a frightened child.*

Look at me, Arthur.

HOUDINI *pulls* CONAN DOYLE*'s hands away from his eyes. It's like ripping the shell off a tortoise.*

You still believe you talked to your son?

CONAN DOYLE *looks slowly up at* HOUDINI.

CONAN DOYLE. Judas.

HOUDINI. You think you're Christ? I think you believe you are.

HOUDINI *starts to pack the $20,000 back into his briefcase.*

CONAN DOYLE. I hope you're pleased with yourself.

HOUDINI. Sure I am. I outsmarted these fakes.

CONAN DOYLE. You're proud of that?

HOUDINI. Had to be done. Two hundred and two exposures, this makes it two hundred and three, since the beginning of this year. Real progress, but I will not rest until the last medium is brought to book. Don't think it doesn't cost me, I am spending thirty thousand a year on this campaign.

I have a wonderful team of investigators out there, working day and night to clean this country. These people are a scourge, a menace to society.

HOUDINI *stands over* MINA*, who is still crumpled on the floor.*

Mrs Crandon, I normally like to have a photograph taken of every medium I expose. A little 'two-shot', as they say in the movie business, would you object?

MINA *says nothing.*

Bess, would you fetch the camera for me?

BESS. I don't like you today, Harry.

BESS *walks quickly offstage.* MINA *gets to her feet. She stands defiantly in front of* HOUDINI.

MINA. You are despicable.

HOUDINI. I am… the greatest illusionist since the dawn of creation. I have been through apple orchards… you don't touch me, there's no deceiving Houdini.

MINA *spits in his face, then walks slowly offstage, swaying like Marilyn Monroe.*

DR CRANDON. We had no choice. There was no chance of producing supernatural phenomena in an atmosphere of such suspicion.

He follows his wife. He turns back to HOUDINI.

Rest assured, your days are numbered.

He goes. HOUDINI *finishes packing away the money.*

HOUDINI (*suddenly friendly, positive*). The offer still stands. Twenty thousand dollars to your Society of Psychical Research, if you can find me a medium who has genuine paranormal powers. But they have to get past me. No one has so far.

He clicks the briefcase shut and smiles as if nothing has happened.

Tomorrow is a special day! My sweet wife and I are doing a show to celebrate our twenty-ninth wedding anniversary. Twenty-nine! My gosh! I have booked you two seats in the front row. Don't feel obliged, but if you can make it, it'd be swell to see you. Arrivederci.

HOUDINI *walks off. The panel of scientists pack up their papers and leave.*

CONAN DOYLE *and* LADY JEAN *are alone.* LADY JEAN *is still hiding amongst the shadows. Long silence, both afraid to speak.*

CONAN DOYLE. Jean.

No response.

Jean.

Nothing.

Dearest Jean…

LADY JEAN. Yes.

CONAN DOYLE. Come here.

She doesn't move.

Please.

LADY JEAN *approaches* CONAN DOYLE. *She looks diffident and scared. She stands in front of her master.*

(*Equally scared, dreading her answer.*) Are you honest?

LADY JEAN *says nothing.*

I need to know. Please! Help me. (*Terribly quiet.*) Save me. Are you honest?

LADY JEAN. Arthur?

CONAN DOYLE. When you write… are you honest?

LADY JEAN. I don't understand.

CONAN DOYLE. Are you truthful?

LADY JEAN. I love you.

CONAN DOYLE. I know you do. Try to look me in the eye.

LADY JEAN *manages to meet* CONAN DOYLE*'s gaze, but it's hard.*

Promise you would never pretend to me.

LADY JEAN. Of course not. Arthur, you know I wouldn't.

CONAN DOYLE (*desperate*). Promise me.

LADY JEAN. I promise.

But she can't look him in the eye. CONAN DOYLE *takes her head in his hands.*

CONAN DOYLE. Look at me. Look at me!

She manages to meet his eye.

I cannot live if we're dishonest with each other.

LADY JEAN (*tears in her eyes*). I would never pretend to you. You know that. I love you.

She tries to kiss him, but still he holds her face at arm's length and examines her.

I love you, Arthur.

LADY JEAN *tries to move* CONAN DOYLE*'s hands.*

You're hurting me… please let go…

But CONAN DOYLE *doesn't loosen his grip. The trial goes on,* CONAN DOYLE *battles with his doubt,* LADY JEAN *continues to suffer but eventually:*

CONAN DOYLE. I believe you. Thank you.

He allows her to collapse into his arms. LADY JEAN*'s tears flow.* CONAN DOYLE *soothes her, stroking her hair.*

Thank you, thank you.

Blackout.

Scene Five

The Ogden Theatre, Denver, Colorado. The following night. A spotlight on BESS.

BESS. Ladies and gentlemen, I, Mademoiselle Beatrice, welcome you to the astonishing world of Houdini, the greatest escapologist since the dawn of creation!

HOUDINI *appears in an explosion of stars and coloured smoke. He strides down to meet his audience.*

HOUDINI. I – am – the – Great – Houdini!!! It's wonderful to be back in Denver, Colorado, the finest city in all the United States of America! What am I talking about! The finest city in the world!! Tonight is a special, special night. On this very day, my sweet wife and I celebrate our twenty-ninth wedding anniversary! Ten thousand, five hundred and eighty-five days of harmony and happiness. (*To* BESS.) Have I been a good boy, honey?

BESS. You've been a very good boy.

HOUDINI. Well, ladies and gentlemen, I've been deliberating what I should buy for my beautiful doll on this special day. What would you like most in the world, honey?

BESS. Sweetheart, I would like a silk gown, smart enough to meet the King of England.

HOUDINI. You shall have one! But I am a man of no sartorial taste, so I'm gonna give you the spondulicks to go out an' buy one yourself.

He starts to produce silver coins from all over his body.

Darling Bess, I need a receptacle for these!

BESS *hands him an empty champagne bucket.* HOUDINI *drops silver coins, one after another, into the bucket. Each coin makes a satisfying clunk as it hits the bottom.*

But you can't carry all these coins around with you, so I'm gonna make transportation of the dough a little easier.

HOUDINI *inverts the bucket and out drops one* huge *silver coin. All the other coins have disappeared.* BESS *starts to walk away with the giant coin and empty bucket.*

Wait a minute, honey, here's a little something you and I might enjoy after the show tonight.

A bottle of champagne appears from nowhere. HOUDINI *drops it into the empty bucket.*

And, sweetheart, you're gonna need something to put round your neck when you meet the King of England.

A jet of flame appears from the tip of HOUDINI*'s fingers and suddenly he's holding a gold necklace. He puts it round his wife's neck.*

With all my love, Mrs Houdini!

BESS. Oh! You're so sweet! I love you, Harry! Thank you so much!

She moves away, giving HOUDINI *room to continue his act.*

HOUDINI. Tonight, in celebration of his wedding anniversary, the Great Houdini… will walk through a solid brick wall!!

Two liveried assistants, JIM *and* FRANZ*, enter carrying a rolled rug on their shoulders. They drop it onto the stage and unroll it.*

A Persian rug, ladies and gentlemen, which I purchased for my little wife in a bazaar in Tehran in nineteen hundred and eight.

The richly coloured 15' by 10' rug now covers most of the stage.

Jim! Franz! Bring on the wall!

Jim and Franz wheel a genuine 10' high, 15' wide brick wall onto the stage, on a trolley.

A solid, single-course brick wall.

JIM *and* FRANZ *wheel it along the edge of the stage, close to the front row of the audience.*

Ladies and gentlemen, have a good look at this. I want you to confirm for me that these are bona fide bricks.

Punters in the front row run their hands over the brickwork.

JIM *and* FRANZ *roll the wall on to the rug. It bisects the rug and sits at 90° to the front row of the stalls.*

And I want you to know this rug is a beautiful thing, but it's just a rug. Why did I put it down? I don't want a single one of you thinking I'm using a trapdoor under the stage. No hocus pocus, no trickery.

JIM *and* FRANZ *bring on two three-sided screens, which they place against, and on directly opposite sides of the wall. Each screen is big enough to hide a single person from the audience's view.*

HOUDINI *takes off his jacket and hands it to* BESS.

And now – with no further ado – Houdini will defy the laws of physics, will do what only ghosts of the spirit world are capable. He will walk through… a solid brick wall!!

BESS *opens the lower panel of the stage-left screen. With a last defiant wave to the audience,* HOUDINI *steps behind the screen.* BESS *closes the lower panel.* HOUDINI *is hidden from view.*

(*From within.*) I'm going! I'm going! I'm through!

BESS *walks round the lower edge of the wall, goes straight to the stage-right screen and opens the lower panel.* HOUDINI *is already there! It has taken him five seconds only to 'walk through' solid brickwork. He steps out, flinging out his arms.*

I am Houdini! The most powerful mystifier since the dawn of mankind!!!

Blackout. Lights up.

The performance is over. CONAN DOYLE *is alone on stage. He examines the brick wall – examines every inch.* HOUDINI *enters – exhausted.*

You came.

No response.

I didn't think you would.

CONAN DOYLE. Nor did I. What you did was unforgivable.

HOUDINI. Jean?

CONAN DOYLE. No.

CONAN DOYLE *taps the wall, listening for anything hollow-sounding.*

So this… is a brick wall?

HOUDINI. It is.

CONAN DOYLE (*tapping his foot on the rug*). And this… is just a rug?

HOUDINI. Purchased in a bazaar in Tehran in nineteen hundred and eight. Yes.

CONAN DOYLE *chooses his words carefully.*

CONAN DOYLE. So what you did was magic?

HOUDINI. Your magic or mine?

CONAN DOYLE. What's the difference?

HOUDINI. Your magic believes I just walked through a brick wall.

CONAN DOYLE. And didn't you?

HOUDINI. No. And if you knew how it was done, you'd be disappointed.

CONAN DOYLE. How did you do it?

HOUDINI *shrugs.*

You won't tell me.

HOUDINI. We have a code of secrecy.

CONAN DOYLE. You have wonderful powers and you still won't admit it. Instead you destroy others with the same gift. You're frightened.

HOUDINI. Of what?

CONAN DOYLE. Of taking yourself seriously.

Silence.

How did you walk through the wall?

No reply.

Be not afeared.

Something about CONAN DOYLE*'s biblical pomposity maddens* HOUDINI.

HOUDINI. The fucking Messiah!

HOUDINI *strides up to the wall. He pulls away the two screens and hurls them offstage. He stands where the stage left screen would have been. He shouts offstage:*

Jim! Jim!

JIM *appears from the wings.*

Release the trap.

JIM *glances at* CONAN DOYLE.

Release the goddamn trap! Now!!

JIM *disappears, he clatters downstairs, he's under the stage.* HOUDINI *leans his hands against the wall and braces himself. He stares aggressively at* CONAN DOYLE.

We hear a bolt being drawn back, then the sound of a trapdoor being released under the stage. At the same second that the trapdoor drops (invisibly, downwards) HOUDINI *drops two feet lower. He bounces at the new height.*

(*Something driven and aggressive in his tone.*) There's a trapdoor under the rug. The centre of the rug is elasticated. When the trapdoor opens, my weight forces the middle of the rug down, creating a gap between the bottom of the wall and the section of the rug I'm standing on. So down I go.

HOUDINI *crouches and climbs through the gap between the bottom of the wall and the rug. He appears instantly on the other side.*

(*Shouted.*) Close it, Jim!

The trapdoor is closed, the rug is flat again. HOUDINI *is standing on 'flat land'.*

Because only the centre of the rug is elasticated, the rest of the rug stays exactly where it is.

Silence.

What did I tell ya? You're disappointed, you can't believe how simple the trick is. You wanted to know, but now you do, everything crumbles to dust. You know why people love my magic? Because they know it's a trick, but a little part of them longs for it not to be, they live in hope that the impossible is possible. What if I really did walk through a brick wall? When I started out, I was just a 'rabbit out of the hat' magician, but now, when I escape from handcuffs and chains and coffins, I become something special. I am Mankind freeing himself from his shackles, I offer liberation. My magic is a beautiful deception, which ain't that dissimilar to your magic, you deceive people too, but it's not beautiful, it's ugly and it's dishonest.

CONAN DOYLE. There is an evil presence in you trying to destroy the good.

HOUDINI. What you gonna do, Arthur? Every trick I perform is just as simple. All based on repetitive practice. When I first climbed under the wall, it took me eleven seconds, now it takes me four. Took me months to perfect. Drop onto the right knee, left knee follows. Right hand, left hand, slightly dislocate right shoulder, introduce into the gap. Flatten body, use left hand and left foot to propel body through gap. Padded shirt across my back to avoid scraping the hell out of my shoulders. Relocate right shoulder. One bounce on the elasticated section of the rug and I'm on my feet. The trapdoor closes and I'm out. I got it down to eight seconds, seven seconds, six seconds and then I stuck, for *weeks*, until I realise, if I use the bounce of the elastic, I'm on my feet two seconds quicker. Four seconds. Every time. All to achieve mystery. Dematerialisation. What d'you say to that?

CONAN DOYLE. I say two things. Firstly I don't believe you use the method you've just shown me at every performance. Of course you need something technical in reserve. You can't be expected to use your powers as a medium day in day out. Your schedule is punishing, occasionally your ability to dematerialise will be diminished, and so for each illusion you need something more basic…

HOUDINI. As backup.

CONAN DOYLE. Exactly.

HOUDINI. You never give up.

CONAN DOYLE. Secondly, there is something destructive and dark in you which you seem unable to resist. There are many in our movement who believe you're in league with the Devil. You've made enemies, my wife included. Jean has received warnings from the other side.

HOUDINI. Is that a threat?

CONAN DOYLE. No. But it's why I came tonight, to advise you to be careful. To warn you as a friend.

Silence, then CONAN DOYLE *crosses the rug, crouches down and feels the elasticated section.*

Very clever.

HOUDINI (*suddenly disillusioned*). Is it? When you do it every night and you strive to be an artist, it feels cheaper and cheaper. Hiding a spare key up your ass. Dislocating your shoulder to give you more slack. Nothing magical about that. Five years I've been exposing fakes. Why d'you think I'm so good at it? Because it takes one to know one, I'm the biggest fake of 'em all. I'm not that interesting when you examine the facts. I have a large collection of keys and a weirdly flexible body that's all.

Short silence.

Tell me the truth. What do you think of me?

CONAN DOYLE. You're extraordinary.

HOUDINI. But am I an artist?

CONAN DOYLE. You're the most powerful medium I've ever met. I can pay you no higher compliment. But like Lucifer, you're dangerous.

HOUDINI. I wrote four books. Good books. Which you still haven't read. Am I right? You still haven't read them, have you?

CONAN DOYLE *says nothing.*

No. My style is highly praised. Brandon wrote in the *New York Times*: 'Houdini's literary style reflects his era – evocative, expressive and exciting.'

CONAN DOYLE. I'm sorry.

HOUDINI. So you keep saying. Arthur, you're the most beautiful magician of them all. Yours is the only magic that matters. You mustn't stop writing.

CONAN DOYLE (*very factual*). I was sent here for one purpose. As a torch-bearer for spiritualism. It was preordained if you like that I should create Sherlock Holmes to get recognition, even friendship, at firesides throughout the world. Holmes was the means to an end. I'm done with him.

HOUDINI. Saddest thing I ever heard. I don't wanna escape from handcuffs any more, you don't wanna write about Sherlock Holmes, we're both…

CONAN DOYLE.… hunting for bigger game.

HOUDINI. Your people are coming for me, Arthur. That's okay, I'm not afraid. Every night they hold séances and pray for my death. When they come, I won't raise a finger to stop them. I'm ready. Ready to join my mother.

CONAN DOYLE. That's what all the fuss and effort is about, Houdini – to try, somehow, to be ready.

CONAN DOYLE *holds out his hand to* HOUDINI.

HOUDINI. You can't have me, Arthur.

CONAN DOYLE. I'm offering to shake hands with my sparring partner. We return to Crowborough tomorrow.

CONAN DOYLE *waits.* HOUDINI *gently parries the outstretched hand and pushes it aside. Equally gently, he places a fist on* CONAN DOYLE*'s chin.*

HOUDINI. Have a good trip. Please give my fond regards to Jean.

CONAN DOYLE. I'll miss you.

HOUDINI. See you on the other side of the veil.

CONAN DOYLE. You *will*. I think you know you will.

HOUDINI. The Tiger! You never give up.

HOUDINI *turns and walks slowly offstage. He lifts his hand and waves without looking back.*

I'll miss you too.

CONAN DOYLE *is left alone. He walks up to the centre of the wall. Yet again he runs his hands over the surface hoping for an answer. Then gently he bangs his head against the brick wall.*

Blackout.

The End.